RULES OF EVIDENCE IN THE UNITED STATES OF AMERICA

Francis DiGiacco, JD

Francis DiGiacco, JD

Rules of Evidence in the United States of America

Photography: Curriculum Technology

Publisher - Channel Custom Publishing 835 5TH Avenue, Suite 205, San Diego, California 92101

Manufactured in the United States of America, 1st edition, Curriculum Technology LLC, 2016.

Rules of Evidence in the USA. A textbook by Curriculum Technology, LLC. San Diego, California. 1st edition 2020

Print edition
ISBN- 978-1-938087-31-8

Experiments and activities derived from this book should be conducted with oversight by, and with direction from, a qualified instructor.

Francis DiGiacco, JD

STUDENT EDITION

This book is an abridged and simplified version of the Federal Rules of Evidence, with additional content provided by the editor and from sources such as the White House, the Department of Justice, The Federal Courts, and the states of Ohio, Connecticut, Missouri, Texas, North Dakota, Texas, Florida, Arizona, and California.

The rules are presented in a textbook format to facilitate presentation and to enhance the student's experience in approaching this material for the first time.

It is not intended to be, nor should it be, used for legal research. This is a guide created for criminal justice students as an entry point into learning about the Rules of Evidence. The Federal Rules of Evidence, and the student's state rules of evidence should be actively used as supplements to the book.

- Relevant cases are referenced at the end of each chapter.
- A brief outline of the Bill of Rights appears at the end of the chapters.
- After the Bill of Rights, you will find the previously mentioned relevant cases posted in the addendum.
- These cases can be discussed in class or briefed as a written assignment.
- A glossary of terms is included.

Francis DiGiacco, JD

Professor DiGiacco teaches in the area of trial advocacy at University of San Diego School of Law. DiGiacco is an associate in the San Diego office of Robbins Geller Rudman & Dowd LLP, where his practice focuses on class action and derivative securities litigation. He clerked for the Honorable Thomas J. Whelan of the Southern District of California and interned at the United States Attorney's Office for the Southern District of California, the California Department of Corporations, and the California Attorney General's Office. DiGiacco joined USD School of Law in 2011.

DiGiacco graduated *cum laude* from the University of San Diego School of Law where he competed nationally in both mock trial and moot court. He received the Thorsnes Outstanding Future Trial Lawyer Award as well as admission into the Order of the Barristers.

FOREWORD

This book is designed to provide the student with an entry point to the rules of evidence. It is designed to be a plain English overview of the background and application of the rules of evidence.

This book is written for those who are entering the field of criminal justice with the goal of becoming a practitioner in the system serving in a role such as a peace officer, court security officer, social services provider, court employee, or correctional officer, as opposed to being an introduction to the legal profession.

You will find in this book a series of cases that have been edited for readability and to help those new to legal issues appreciate the relationship of the rules of evidence with case law and procedural law.

It is the hope of the publisher that you will find this book helpful. It is a compilation of material garnered from various states and the federal government. As you use the book you should also reference your particular state's laws and procedures.

The editorial team would like to acknowledge the legislators, executive, and judiciary of the states of Ohio, Connecticut, Missouri, Texas, North Dakota, Texas, Florida, Arizona, and California as excerpts of their rules and other related materials are incorporated throughout the content.

Also, the editorial team acknowledges and assigns attribution to the Department of Justice, the Supreme Court, the National Archives, the US Senate and House of Representatives, and the White House for select excerpts incorporated into this book.

Francis DiGiacco, JD

CHAPTER 1 - OVERVIEW OF THE RULES OF EVIDENCE

INTRODUCTION

The rules of evidence should be construed so as to administer every proceeding fairly, eliminate unjustifiable expense and delay, and promote the development of evidence, to the end of ascertaining the truth and securing a just determination. In this chapter, we will define the rules of evidence and outline several preliminary provisions for the rules including how evidence is presented, preliminary questions, and judicial notice.

The rules address the legal requirements of the admission of evidence in a courtroom during a trial or other judicial proceeding.

Occasionally, the term *"rules of evidence"* is misconstrued to mean the forensic requirements for physical evidence. In this context, the rules of evidence are about the admission of evidence from a legal perspective, including evidence relating to privilege, hearsay, and best evidence.

As you study these rules, think of them in terms of 'rulings', or how should a judge rule on evidence presented by the defense and prosecution. Some matters are guided by case law, and others are left to the discretion to the judge. The rules of evidence also preserve a pathway to appeals, should the rules not be followed.

The rules of evidence apply to proceedings in courts of the United States. Each of the states has evidentiary rules for their courts as do the Federal Courts.

Knowing the rules of evidence will enable you to understand how different types of evidence are admitted to court.

OBJECTIVES

1. Define Rules of Evidence and what function they have in courtroom proceedings
2. Identify how rulings are made
3. List two criteria for judicial notice to be taken

KEY TERMS

- *Civil case* - A civil action or proceeding
- *Criminal case* - A criminal case proceeding
- *Public Office* - Includes any public agency
- *Record* - A written account of the proceedings in a case, including all pleadings, evidence, and exhibits submitted in the course of the case. Includes a memorandum, report, or data compilation

EVIDENCE IN A CRIMINAL PROCEEDING

Evidence is defined as any species of proof legally presented at trial through witnesses, records, documents, exhibits or other physical objects by which any fact in dispute is established or disproved. The object of all evidence is to inform the trier of fact, either the judge or the jury, of the material, relevant facts so that the truth may be elicited, and a fair determination of the controversy be reached. Thus, the judge or jury must decide a case only on the evidence introduced or presented during the trial.

The court must be mindful that its personal knowledge of facts regarding the case such as intersections of business or personal is not to be considered. The only facts that a court may consider are those elicited from the witness stand or through other evidentiary channels.

The party that seeks the admission of particular evidence whether through testimony or physical objects is responsible for securing its presence at trial. This can be done through subpoena to secure the attendance of a person or production of documents.

https://www.courts.mo.gov/file/11%20Bench%20Book%20-%20Chapter%20XI.pdf

RULINGS ON EVIDENCE

According to the Federal Judicial Center, the presentation of evidence is subject to rules that are designed to ensure that only reliable and relevant evidence is admitted. Sometimes, the rules even exclude reliable and relevant evidence to protect other important interests.

In a jury trial, a lawyer will sometimes break one of these rules of evidence, either accidentally or on purpose, and will try to present evidence to the jury that it should not hear.

If a lawyer believes the testimony that an opposing lawyer asked a witness for is improper, the lawyer may object to it and may ask the judge to instruct the witness not to answer the question. If the witness has already answered, the lawyer may still object and ask the judge to tell the jury to disregard what the witness said. The judge can either sustain the objection and do as the objecting lawyer requests or overrule it and permit the testimony. When an objection is made, the judge alone decides whether the testimony is admissible.

Occasionally, the judge and the lawyers for both sides have a conference at the bench (called a sidebar) out of the jury's hearing but with the court reporter present to record what they say. At other times, they might confer in the judge's chambers, or office.

Often, they are discussing whether a certain piece of evidence is admissible. The court does not want the jurors to hear this discussion because they might hear something that cannot be admitted into evidence and that might prejudice them in favor of one side or the other.

There are several rules guiding the process for the introduction or exclusion of evidence as follows:

Preserving a claim of error:

A party may claim error in a ruling to admit or exclude evidence only if the error affects a substantial right of the party and, if the ruling admits evidence, a party, on the record:

- Timely objects or moves to strike; and
- States the specific ground, unless it was apparent from the context;
- Or if the ruling excludes evidence, a party informs the court of its substance by an offer of proof, unless the substance was apparent from the context.

Not needing to renew and objection or offer of proof:

Once the court rules definitively on the record, either before or at trial, a party need not renew an objection or offer of proof to preserve a claim of error for appeal.

Courts statement about the ruling; Directing an offer of proof

The court may make any statement about the character or form of the evidence, the objection made, and the ruling. The court may direct that an offer of proof be made in question and answer form.

Preventing the jury from hearing inadmissible evidence

To the extent practicable, the court must conduct a jury trial so that inadmissible evidence is not suggested to the jury by any means.

Taking notice of plain error

A court may take notice of a plain error affecting a substantial right, even if the claim of error was not properly preserved.

PRELIMINARY QUESTIONS

Preliminary questions are necessary to determine the qualifications of a person to be a witness, the existence of a privilege, or the admissibility of evidence. In general, the court must be the decider of any preliminary question about whether a witness is qualified, a privilege exists, or evidence is admissible. In so deciding, the court is not bound by evidence rules, except for those on privilege.

Other than privilege issues, the judge is not bound by the rules of evidence at this point, although ironically, the rules of evidence are where that freedom for the judge to decide is established. When the relevance of evidence depends on whether a fact exists, proof must be introduced sufficient to support a finding that the fact does exist. The court may admit the proposed evidence on the condition that the proof will be introduced later.

The court must conduct any hearing on a preliminary question so that the jury cannot hear it if the hearing involves the admissibility of a confession, a defendant in a criminal case is a witness and so requests, or justice so requires. By testifying on a preliminary question, a defendant in a criminal case does not become subject to cross-examination on other issues in the case.

The evidence relevant to weight and credibility rule does not limit a party's right to introduce before the jury evidence that is relevant to the weight or credibility of other evidence.

LIMITING EVIDENCE THAT IS NOT ADMISSIBLE AGAINST OTHER PARTIES OR FOR OTHER PURPOSES

If the court admits evidence that is admissible against a party or for a purpose—but not against another party or for another purpose, the court, on timely request, must restrict the evidence to its proper scope and instruct the jury accordingly.

"RULE OF COMPLETENESS" - REMAINDER OF OR RELATED WRITINGS OR RECORDED STATEMENTS

If a party introduces all or part of a writing or recorded statement, an adverse party may require the introduction, at that time, of any other part - or any other writing or recorded statement that in fairness ought to be considered at the same time. This is commonly referred to as the Rule of Completeness.

JUDICIAL NOTICE

This rule governs judicial notice of an adjudicative fact only, not a legislative fact. The court may judicially notice a fact that is not subject to reasonable dispute because it:

- Is generally known within the trial court's territorial jurisdiction; or
- Can be accurately and readily determined from sources whose accuracy cannot reasonably be questioned.

The court may take judicial notice on its own, or it must take it if a party requests it and provides the court with the necessary information. Judicial notice can be taken at any time during a proceeding.

On timely request, a party is entitled to be heard on the propriety of taking judicial notice and the nature of the fact to be noticed. If the court takes judicial notice before notifying a party, the party, on request, is still entitled to be heard.

In a civil case, the court must instruct the jury to accept the noticed fact as conclusive. In a criminal case, the court must instruct the jury that it may or may not accept the noticed fact as conclusive.

Examples of facts that are subject to judicial notice include dates on a calendar, mathematical principles, laws of physics, systems of measurement, laws of other states or countries, judicial decisions in other cases, and the locations of local businesses.

ASSIGNMENTS

CASE BRIEF

Read and discuss case 1 - Privilege - United States of America vs. Leroy Waters, et al.

ACTIVITY

1. Create a list of five things that might qualify for judicial notice. Explain your answer.

2. Write a list of preliminary questions for a witness who observed a traffic accident.

CHAPTER 2 - RELEVANCE AND ITS LIMITS

INTRODUCTION

"*Relevant evidence*" means evidence having any tendency in reason, to prove or disprove any disputed fact that is of consequence to the determination of the action and establishing the disputed fact as more probable or less probable than it would be without the evidence. This includes evidence relevant to the credibility of a witness or hearsay declarant.

OBJECTIVES

1. To assess the difference between relevant and Irrelevant evidence
2. To establish that irrelevant evidence is not admissible
3. To evaluate how evidence is determined relevant

KEY TERMS

- ***Relevant evidence*** - Evidence and testimony directly relating to the issues disputed or discussed
- ***Character*** - A person's credit, character, honor, reputation, and/or good name

TEST FOR RELEVANT EVIDENCE

Relevance is the first step in any analysis of whether evidence is admissible. Evidence is relevant if it has any tendency to make a fact more or less probable than it would be without the evidence, and the fact is of consequence in determining the action. The evidence does not need to prove the fact to be relevant.

Relevant evidence is admissible unless any of the following provides otherwise:

- The United States Constitution
- A federal statute
- The rules of evidence
- Other rules prescribed by the Supreme Court

NOTE: Irrelevant evidence is not admissible.

EXCLUDING RELEVANT EVIDENCE FOR PREJUDICE, CONFUSION, WASTE OF TIME, OR OTHER REASONS

The court may exclude relevant evidence if its probative value is substantially outweighed by a danger of one or more of the following: unfair prejudice, confusing the issues, misleading the jury, undue delay, wasting time, or needlessly presenting cumulative evidence.

CHARACTER EVIDENCE; CRIMES OR OTHER ACTS

Evidence of a person's character or character trait is not admissible to prove that on a particular occasion the person acted in accordance with the character or trait. A defendant may offer evidence of a pertinent character trait of his own, and if the evidence is admitted, the prosecutor may offer evidence to rebut it. Generally, a defendant may offer evidence of a pertinent character trait of an alleged victim, and if the evidence is admitted, the prosecutor may offer evidence to rebut it or offer evidence of the defendant's same trait. In a homicide case, the prosecutor may offer evidence of the alleged victim's character for peacefulness to rebut evidence that the victim was the first aggressor.

Evidence of a witness's character may be admitted, especially as it relates to the witness's character for truthfulness. Evidence of a crime, wrong, or other act is not admissible to prove a person's character to show that on a particular occasion the person acted in accordance with that character. However, a witness's prior felony convictions, under certain circumstances, may be admitted as evidence of the witness's character for truthfulness. This evidence may be admissible for another purpose, such as proving motive, opportunity, intent, preparation, plan, knowledge, identity, absence of mistake, or lack of accident. On request by a defendant in a criminal case, the prosecutor must provide reasonable notice of the general nature of any such evidence that the prosecutor intends to offer at trial and do so before trial or during trial if the court, for good cause, excuses lack of pretrial notice.

Character may be proven by either or both of two things, reputation or opinion, or specific instances of conduct. When evidence of a person's character or a character trait is admissible, it may be proved by testimony about the person's reputation or by testimony in the form of an opinion. On cross-examination of the character witness, the court may allow an inquiry into relevant specific instances of the person's conduct.

When a person's character or a character trait is an essential element of a charge, claim, or defense, the character or trait may also be proved by relevant specific instances of the person's conduct.

HABIT AND ROUTINE PRACTICE

Evidence of a person's habit or an organization's routine practice may be admitted to prove that on a particular occasion the person or organization acted in accordance with the habit or routine practice. The court may admit this evidence regardless of whether it is corroborated or whether there was an eyewitness.

COMPROMISE OFFERS AND NEGOTIATIONS

Prohibited uses

Evidence of the following is not admissible on behalf of any party, either to prove or disprove the validity or amount of a disputed claim or to impeach by a prior inconsistent statement or a contradiction:

- Furnishing, promising, or offering, or accepting, promising to accept, or offering to accept—a valuable consideration in compromising or attempting to compromise the claim; and

- Conduct or a statement made during compromise negotiations about the claim, except when offered in a criminal case and when the negotiations related to a claim by a public office in the exercise of its regulatory, investigative, or enforcement authority.

The court may admit this evidence for another purpose, such as proving a witness's bias or prejudice, negating a contention of undue delay, or proving an effort to obstruct a criminal investigation or prosecution.

OFFERS TO PAY MEDICAL AND SIMILAR EXPENSES

Evidence of furnishing, promising to pay, or offering to pay medical, hospital, or similar expenses resulting from an injury is not admissible to prove liability for the injury.

PLEAS, PLEA DISCUSSIONS, AND RELATED STATEMENTS

A plea, simply put, is an answer to a question. In the criminal courtroom environment, a plea is a response to a criminal charge. The defendant will answer to individual allegations, put forth in a complaint by denying or admitting each charge with a plea of guilty, not guilty, or no contest. This section will address the rules concerning pleas, rather than the procedural issues.

In a criminal case, evidence of the following is not admissible against the defendant who made the plea or participated in the plea discussions:

- A guilty plea that was later withdrawn
- Nolo contendere (no contest) plea
- A statement made during a proceeding on either of those pleas
- A statement made during plea discussions with an attorney for the prosecuting authority if the discussions did not result in a guilty plea or they resulted in a later-withdrawn guilty plea.
- There are a few exceptions to this rule. The court may admit a statement:
- In any proceeding in which another statement made during the same plea or plea discussions has been introduced, if in fairness, the statements ought to be considered together; or
- In a criminal proceeding for perjury or false statement, if the defendant made the statement under oath, on the record, and with counsel present.

LIABILITY INSURANCE

Evidence that a person was or was not insured against liability is not admissible to prove whether the person acted negligently or otherwise wrongfully. But the court may admit this evidence for another purpose, such as proving a witness's bias or prejudice or proving agency, ownership, or control.

SEX OFFENSE CASES: THE VICTIM'S SEXUAL BEHAVIOR OR PREDISPOSITION

The courts have taken steps to find a fine balance between protecting victims of sex offenses and protecting the rights of the accused. Evidence is not admissible in a civil or criminal proceeding involving alleged sexual misconduct if the evidence is offered to prove that a victim engaged in other sexual behavior, or the evidence offered to prove a victim's sexual predisposition.

The court may admit the following evidence in a criminal case:

- Evidence of specific instances of a victim's sexual behavior, if offered to prove that someone other than the defendant was the source of semen, injury, or other physical evidence;

- Evidence of specific instances of a victim's sexual behavior with respect to the person accused of the sexual misconduct, if offered by the defendant to prove consent or if offered by the prosecutor; and

- Evidence whose exclusion would violate the defendant's constitutional rights.

ADMISSIBILITY

If a party intends to offer evidence, the party must file a motion that specifically describes the evidence and states the purpose for which it is to be offered, serve the motion on all parties, and in some states, notify the victim or, when appropriate, the victim's guardian or representative.

Before admitting evidence under this rule, the court must conduct an *in camera* hearing and give the victim and parties a right to attend and be heard. Unless the court orders otherwise, the motion, related materials, and the record of the hearing must be and remain sealed.

If the prosecutor intends to offer this evidence, the prosecutor must disclose it to the defendant, including witnesses' statements or a summary of the expected testimony. The prosecutor must do so in advance of the trial or at a later time that the court allows for good cause, within the timeframes allowed by the jurisdiction. This rule does not limit the admission or consideration of evidence under any other rule.

"Sexual assault" means a crime under federal law or under state law involving:

1. Contact, without consent, between any part of the defendant's body—or an object—and another person's genitals or anus;

2. Contact, without consent, between the defendant's genitals or anus and any part of another person's body;

3. Deriving sexual pleasure or gratification from inflicting death, bodily injury, or physical pain on another person; or

4. An attempt or conspiracy to engage in conduct described in subparagraphs 1– 4.

SIMILAR CRIMES IN CHILD-MOLESTATION CASES

In a criminal case in which a defendant is accused of child molestation, the court may admit evidence that the defendant committed any other child molestation. The evidence may be considered on any matter to which it is relevant.

If the prosecutor intends to offer this evidence, the prosecutor must disclose it to the defendant, including witnesses' statements or a summary of the expected testimony. The prosecutor must do so within the time frame authorized by the jurisdiction or at a later time that the court allows for good cause. This does not limit the admission or consideration of evidence under any other rule.

Under Federal Rules:

- *"Child"* means a person below the age of 14
- *"Child molestation"* means a crime under federal law or under state law, consistent with the following elements:

   – Any conduct prohibited by 18 U.S.C. Chapter 109A (Sexual Abuse) and committed with a child

   – Any conduct prohibited by 18 U.S.C. Chapter 110 (Sexual Exploitation and other abuse of children)

   – Contact between any part of the defendant's body, or an object, and a child's genitals or anus;

   – Contact between the defendant's genitals or anus and any part of a child's body

   – Deriving sexual pleasure or gratification from inflicting death, bodily injury, or physical pain on a child; or

   – An attempt or conspiracy to engage in conduct described in the preceding sections

SIMILAR ACTS IN CIVIL CASES INVOLVING SEXUAL ASSAULT OR CHILD MOLESTATION

Permitted uses

In a civil case involving a claim for relief based on a party's alleged sexual assault or child molestation, the court may admit evidence that the party committed any other sexual assault or child molestation.

Disclosure to the opponent

If a party intends to offer this evidence, the party must disclose it to the party against whom it will be offered, including witnesses' statements or a summary of the expected testimony. The party must do so at least 15 days before trial or at a later time that the court allows for good cause.

Effect on other rules

This rule does not limit the admission or consideration of evidence under any other rule.

ASSIGNMENTS

CASE BRIEF

Read and discuss case 2 - Hearsay - Ohio v. Roberts

ACTIVITY

1. The court may exclude relevant evidence if its probative value is substantially outweighed by a danger of one or more of the following: unfair prejudice, confusing the issues, misleading the jury, undue delay, wasting time, or needlessly presenting cumulative evidence. Write examples of what these might be.

2. Character may be proven by either or both of two things, reputation or opinion, or specific instances of conduct. Identify a court case where this might come into play and explain how character was used by defense or prosecution.

CHAPTER 3 - PRIVILEGE IN GENERAL

INTRODUCTION

Privileged communication refers to statements made by people within protected relationships (e.g., husband and wife, attorney and client, doctor and patient) that the law shields from compelled disclosure on the witness stand. The common law, as interpreted by United States courts in the light of reason and experience, governs a claim of privilege unless any of the following provides otherwise:

- The United States Constitution
- A federal statute
- Rules prescribed by the Supreme Court

But in a civil case, state law governs privilege regarding a claim or defense for which state law supplies the rule of decision.

OBJECTIVES

1. Compare and contrast privileged communications of relationships such as attorney/client, physician/patient
2. Identify exceptions to privilege rules and examine why they exist

KEY TERMS

- ***Attorney-client privilege*** - The protection that applicable law provides for confidential attorney-client communications

- ***In camera*** - Latin, meaning in a judge's chambers. Often means outside the presence of a jury and the public. In private.

- ***Work-product protection*** - The protection that applicable law provides for tangible material (or its intangible equivalent) prepared in anticipation of litigation or for trial

ATTORNEY-CLIENT PRIVILEGE AND WORK PRODUCT; LIMITATIONS ON WAIVER

The following provisions apply, in the circumstances set out, to disclosure of a communication or information covered by the attorney-client privilege or work-product protection.

DISCLOSURE MADE IN A FEDERAL PROCEEDING OR TO A FEDERAL OFFICE OR AGENCY; SCOPE OF A WAIVER

When the disclosure is made in a federal proceeding or to a federal governmental office or agency and waives the attorney-client privilege or work-product protection, the waiver extends to an undisclosed communication or information in a federal or state proceeding only if:

- The waiver is intentional
- The disclosed and undisclosed communications or information concern the same subject matter
- They ought in fairness to be considered together

Inadvertent disclosure

When made in a federal proceeding or to a federal office or agency, the disclosure does not operate as a waiver in a federal or state proceeding if:

- The disclosure is inadvertent
- The holder of the privilege or protection took reasonable steps to prevent disclosure
- The holder promptly took reasonable steps to rectify the error

Disclosure made in state proceedings

When the disclosure is made in a state proceeding and is not the subject of a state- court order concerning waiver, the disclosure does not operate as a waiver in a federal proceeding if the disclosure:

- Would not be a waiver under this rule if it had been made in a federal proceeding
- Is not a waiver under the law of the state where the disclosure occurred

Controlling effect of a court order

A federal court may order that the privilege or protection is not waived by disclosure connected with the litigation pending before the court, in which event the disclosure is also not a waiver in any other federal or state proceeding.

Controlling effect of a party agreement

An agreement on the effect of disclosure in a federal proceeding is binding only on the parties to the agreement, unless it is incorporated into a court order.

OTHER PRIVILEGED COMMUNICATIONS

Although jurisdictions may vary on interpretation or rules, privilege generally encompasses similar relationships. The following persons shall not be compelled to testify in certain respects:

Attorney

An attorney, concerning a communication made to the attorney by a client in that relation or concerning the attorney's advice to a client, except that the attorney may testify by express consent of the client or, if the client is deceased, by the express consent of the surviving spouse or the executor or administrator of the estate of the deceased client. However, if the client voluntarily reveals the substance of attorney- client communications in a non-privileged context or is deemed to have waived any testimonial privilege, the attorney may be compelled to testify on the same subject.

Physician

A physician or a dentist concerning a communication made to the physician or dentist by a patient in that relation or the physician's or dentist's advice to a patient.

Cleric

A cleric, when the cleric remains accountable to the authority of that cleric's church, denomination, or sect, concerning a confession made, or any information confidentially communicated, to the cleric for a religious counseling purpose in the cleric's professional character.

The cleric may testify by express consent of the person making the communication, except when the disclosure of the information is in violation of a sacred trust and except that, if the person voluntarily testifies or is deemed to have waived any testimonial privilege, the cleric may be compelled to testify on the same subject except when disclosure of the information is in violation of a sacred trust.

Sacred trust means a confession or confidential communication made to a cleric in the cleric's ecclesiastical capacity in the course of discipline enjoined by the church to which the cleric belongs, if both of the following apply:

- The confession or confidential communication was made directly to the cleric.

- The confession or confidential communication was made in the manner and context that places the cleric specifically and strictly under a level of confidentiality that is considered inviolate by canon law or church doctrine.

Spousal privilege

Husband or wife, concerning any communication made by one to the other, or an act done by either in the presence of the other, during covertures, unless the communication was made, or act done, in the known presence or hearing of a third person competent to be a witness; and such rule is the same if the marital relation has ceased to exist.

The Ninth Circuit recognizes that the marital privilege doctrine is comprised of two distinct privileges:

1) the anti-marital facts privilege and

2) the marital communications privilege. See United States v. White, 974 F.2d 1135,1137 (9th Cir. 1992).

The anti-marital facts privilege prohibits one spouse from testifying against another during the length of the marriage. The marital communications privilege bars testimony concerning statements privately communicated between spouses. Therefore, while the dissolution of the marriage terminates the privilege under the anti-marital facts privilege, if the communication was confidential and occurred during the marriage it would still be privileged. *Pereira v. United States, 347 U.S. 1, 6 (1954); United States v. Marashi, 913 F.2d 724, 729-30 (9th Cir. 1990).*

Either spouse may assert the privilege as long as there is a valid contract of marriage in existence at the time of the proffered testimony. *Marashi, 913 F.2d at 729-30.* However, it is important to remember that whereas the dissolution of the marriage terminates the privilege under the anti-marital facts privilege, this is not the case with the confidential communications privilege. Confidential communications during the marriage are always privileged (unless certain public policy grounds dictate otherwise, see discussion infra).

In order to assert the privilege a timely objection must be made to the allegedly privileged communication. See *United States v. Figueroa-Paz, 468 F.2d 1055, 1057 (9th Cir. 1972)* (finding that when the defendant "failed to object to his wife's testimony as to his communications when it was offered," he waived the privilege); *United States v. Montgomery, 384 F.3d 1050, 1057 (9th Cir. 2004)* ("[T]he marital communications privilege will be waived if an objection is not timely made.").

Exceptions:

- **Divorce** - Divorce removes the bar of incompetency and terminates the privilege. *Garcia-Jaramillo v. INS, 604 F.2d 1236, 1238 (9th Cir. 1979).* Once divorced, a spouse may testify against his or her spouse.

- **If Spouse is Victim of Crime** - The anti-marital facts privilege does not apply where the spouse or his or her children are the victims of a crime carried out by the other spouse. White, 974 F.2d at 1138.

Marital Communications Privilege

There are several well settled limitations regarding the applicability of the marital communications privilege. First, the privilege does not apply to communications not intended to be private, for example, if a third party was present at the time of the communication. *Pereira, 347 U.S. at 6.* Second, the privilege does not apply to communications which the speaker intended to be conveyed to a third party. Third, the privilege extends only to utterances, not to acts. Fourth, the privilege applies only to communications that were confidential and occurred during the marriage. Fifth, the privilege may be waived. *Matter of B, 51 I&N Dec. at 741.* Lastly, communications relating to present or future crimes are not privileged. *White, 974 F.2d at 1138.*

The Ninth Circuit has also commented that, *"the marital communications privilege must be narrowly construed because it obstructs the truth seeking process."*

Source: https://www.justice.gov/sites/default/files/eoir/legacy/2014/08/15/ marital-privledge-standard.pdf

Counselor

A school guidance counselor who holds a valid educator license from the state board of education as a licensed professional clinical counselor, licensed professional counselor, social worker, independent social worker, marriage and family therapist or independent marriage and family therapist, as a social work assistant concerning a confidential communication received from a client in that relation or the person's advice to a client unless any of the following applies:

- The communication or advice indicates clear and present danger to the client or other persons. For the purposes of this division, cases in which there are indications of present or past child abuse or neglect of the client constitute a clear and present danger.
- The client gives express consent to the testimony.

- If the client is deceased, the surviving spouse or the executor or administrator of the estate of the deceased client gives express consent.

- The client voluntarily testifies, in which case the school guidance counselor may be compelled to testify on the same subject.

- The court *in camera* determines that the information communicated by the client is not germane to the counselor-client, marriage and family therapist-client, or social worker-client relationship.

- A court, in an action brought against a school, its administration, or any of its personnel by the client, rules after an *in camera* inspection that the testimony of the school guidance counselor is relevant to that action.

In most jurisdictions, nothing in any exception noted above relieves a school guidance counselor from the requirement to report information concerning child abuse or neglect.

Mediators in domestic relations

A mediator acting under a mediation order in any proceeding for divorce, dissolution, legal separation, annulment, or the allocation of parental rights and responsibilities for the care of children, in any action or proceeding, other than a criminal, delinquency, child abuse, child neglect, or dependent child action or proceeding, that is brought by or against either parent who takes part in mediation in accordance with the order and that pertains to the mediation process, to any information discussed or presented in the mediation process, to the allocation of parental rights and responsibilities for the care of the parents' children, or to the awarding of parenting time rights in relation to their children.

This list is not all-inclusive, and there are numerous exceptions to the rules that vary between jurisdictions.

ASSIGNMENTS

CASE BRIEF

Read and discuss case 3 - Spousal Privilege - In the United States District Court for the District of Hawaii United States of America, plaintiff, vs. Perry Artates, defendant. Waters et al.

ACTIVITY

1. Create a list of communications that are protected by privilege. Create examples and explain your answer.

2. Explain the importance of attorney-client privilege and how it is crucial to protecting the integrity of the justice system.

CHAPTER 4 - WITNESSES

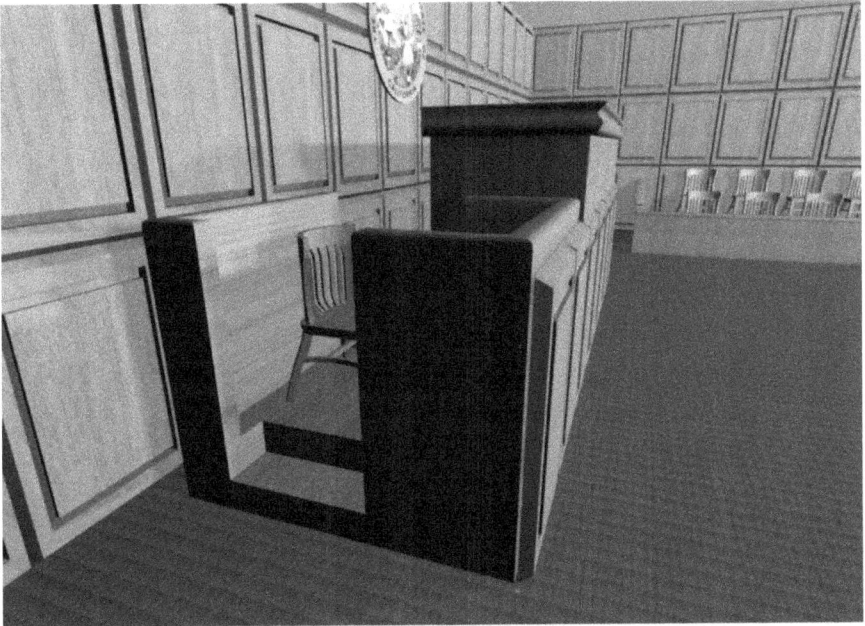

INTRODUCTION

The general rule regarding witnesses is that a person may be considered competent to testify if he or she is able to perceive, remember, and communicate, and believes that they are morally obligated to tell the truth. Legislatures set a standard of competency for witnesses in all cases. In the case of young children, the court must assess whether the child is competent to testify.

OBJECTIVES

1. Evaluate what constitutes competency as it relates to witnesses in a criminal proceeding

2. Identify and define prohibited testimony

KEY TERMS

Witness - A person who has knowledge of an event by seeing it

Pendency - A state of being undecided, the state of an action after it has begun, and before it has been decided

NEED FOR PERSONAL KNOWLEDGE

A witness may testify to a matter only if evidence is introduced sufficient to support a finding that the witness has personal knowledge of the matter. Evidence to prove personal knowledge may consist of the witness's own testimony. This rule does not apply to a witness's expert testimony.

OATH OR AFFIRMATION TO TESTIFY TRUTHFULLY

Before testifying, a witness must give an oath or affirmation to testify truthfully. It must be in a form designed to impress that duty on the witness's conscience. The oath or affirmation may be given substantially in the following form; "Do you solemnly swear to tell the truth, the whole truth, and nothing but the truth? So help you God." A person must be allowed to make an affirmation instead of taking an oath, by substituting the word "affirm" for the word "swear" and substituting the phrase "under the pains and penalties of perjury" for the phrase "so help you God."

INTERPRETER

An interpreter must be qualified and must give an oath or affirmation to make a true translation.

JUDGE'S COMPETENCY AS A WITNESS

The presiding judge may not testify as a witness at the trial. A party need not object to preserve the issue.

JUROR'S COMPETENCY AS A WITNESS

A juror may not testify as a witness before the other jurors at the trial. If a juror is called to testify, the court must give a party an opportunity to object outside the jury's presence.

DURING AN INQUIRY INTO THE VALIDITY OF A VERDICT OR INDICTMENT

Prohibited Testimony or Other Evidence

During an inquiry into the validity of a verdict or indictment, a juror may not testify about any statement made or incident that occurred during the jury's deliberations; the effect of anything on that juror's or another juror's vote; or any juror's mental processes concerning the verdict or indictment. The court may not receive a juror's affidavit or evidence of a juror's statement on these matters.

Exceptions

A juror may testify about whether:

- Extraneous prejudicial information was improperly brought to the jury's attention;
- An outside influence was improperly brought to bear on any juror; or
- A mistake was made in entering the verdict on the verdict form.

WHO MAY IMPEACH A WITNESS

Any party, including the party that called the witness, may attack the witness's credibility.

A WITNESS'S CHARACTER FOR TRUTHFULNESS OR UNTRUTHFULNESS

Reputation or opinion evidence

A witness's credibility may be attacked or supported by testimony about the witness's reputation for having a character for truthfulness or untruthfulness, or by testimony in the form of an opinion about that character. But evidence of truthful character is admissible only after the witness's character for truthfulness has been attacked.

Specific instances of conduct

Except for a criminal conviction, extrinsic evidence is not admissible to prove specific instances of a witness's conduct to attack or support the witness's character for truthfulness. But the court may, on cross-examination, allow them to be inquired into if they are probative of the character for truthfulness or untruthfulness of:

- The witness
- Another witness whose character the witness being cross-examined has testified about

By testifying on another matter, a witness does not waive any privilege against self- incrimination for testimony that relates only to the witness's character for truthfulness.

Impeachment by evidence of a criminal conviction

The following rules apply to attacking a witness's character for truthfulness by evidence of a criminal conviction for a crime that, in the convicting jurisdiction, was punishable by death or by imprisonment for more than one year, the evidence:

- Must be admitted, subject to rules regarding evidence for prejudice, confusion, or waste of time, in a civil case or in a criminal case in which the witness is not a defendant; and

- Must be admitted in a criminal case in which the witness is a defendant, if the probative value of the evidence outweighs its prejudicial effect to that defendant; and

- For any crime regardless of the punishment, the evidence must be admitted if the court can readily determine that establishing the elements of the crime required proving, or the witness's admitting, a dishonest act or false statement.

Limit on using evidence after 10 years

This limit applies in Federal court if more than 10 years have passed since the witness's conviction or release from confinement for it, whichever is later. State courts may vary on this time limit. Evidence of the conviction is admissible only if its probative value, supported by specific facts and circumstances, substantially outweighs its prejudicial effect; and the proponent gives an adverse party reasonable written notice of the intent to use it so that the party has a fair opportunity to contest its use.

Effect of a pardon, annulment, or certificate of rehabilitation

Evidence of a conviction is not admissible if the conviction has been the subject of a pardon, annulment, certificate of rehabilitation, or other equivalent procedure based on a finding that the person has been rehabilitated, and the person has not been convicted of a later crime punishable by death or by imprisonment for more than one year; or the conviction has been the subject of a pardon, annulment, or other equivalent procedure based on a finding of innocence.

Juvenile adjudications

Evidence of a juvenile adjudication is admissible under this rule only if it is offered in a criminal case and:

- The adjudication was of a witness other than the defendant

- An adult's conviction for that offense would be admissible to attack the adult's credibility
- Admitting the evidence is necessary to fairly determine guilt or innocence

Pendency of an appeal

A conviction that satisfies this rule is admissible even if an appeal is pending. Evidence of the pendency is also admissible.

RELIGIOUS BELIEFS OR OPINIONS

Evidence of a witness's religious beliefs or opinions is not admissible to attack or support the witness's credibility.

MODE AND ORDER OF EXAMINING WITNESSES AND PRESENTING EVIDENCE

Control by the court; purposes

The court should exercise reasonable control over the mode and order of examining witnesses and presenting evidence so as to; make those procedures effective for determining the truth; avoid wasting time; and protect witnesses from harassment or undue embarrassment.

Scope of cross-examination

Cross-examination should not go beyond the subject matter of the direct examination and matters affecting the witness's credibility. The court may allow inquiry into additional matters as if on direct examination.

Leading questions

Leading questions should not be used on direct examination except as necessary to develop the witness's testimony. Ordinarily, the court should allow leading questions on cross-examination; and when a party calls a hostile witness, an adverse party, or a witness identified with an adverse party.

WRITING USED TO REFRESH A WITNESS'S MEMORY

There are two different situations that arise when a witness cannot immediately recall the facts but is able to do so through the aid of a writing. The rules applying to them in trial are different.

The first of these is known as present recollection refreshed and requires that the witness be able to testify independently without the writing, after refreshing his memory. However, when a witness is unable to testify from memory, the document may be admitted into evidence if the witness testifies as to its accuracy. The witness must be able to testify either that he made the writing or that at some point in the past he knew it to be correct. This particular exception has little practical use because the writing itself would generally be admissible as a business record, or under some other hearsay exception.

Scope

This rule gives an adverse party certain options when a witness uses a writing to refresh memory while testifying; or before testifying, if the court decides that justice requires the party to have those options.

Adverse party's options; Deleting unrelated matter

In a criminal case, an adverse party is entitled to have the writing produced at the hearing, to inspect it, to cross-examine the witness about it, and to introduce in evidence any portion that relates to the witness's testimony. If the producing party claims that the writing includes unrelated matter, the court must examine the writing *in camera*, delete any unrelated portion, and order that the rest be delivered to the adverse party. Any portion deleted over objection must be preserved for the record.

Failure to produce or deliver the writing

If a writing is not produced or is not delivered as ordered, the court may issue any appropriate order. But if the prosecution does not comply in a criminal case, the court must strike the witness's testimony or, if justice so requires, declare a mistrial.

WITNESS'S PRIOR STATEMENT

Showing or disclosing the statement during examination

When examining a witness about the witness's prior statement, a party need not show it or disclose its contents to the witness. But the party must, on request, show it or disclose its contents to an adverse party's attorney.

Extrinsic evidence of a prior inconsistent statement

Extrinsic evidence of a witness's prior inconsistent statement is admissible only if the witness is given an opportunity to explain or deny the statement and an adverse party is given an opportunity to examine the witness about it, or if justice so requires. This opportunity to explain does not apply to an opposing party's statement.

COURT'S CALLING OR EXAMINING A WITNESS

Calling

The court may call a witness on its own or at a party's request. Each party is entitled to cross-examine the witness.

Examining

The court may examine a witness regardless of who calls the witness.

Objections

A party may object to the court's calling or examining a witness either at that time or at the next opportunity when the jury is not present.

EXCLUDING WITNESSES

At a party's request, the court must order witnesses excluded so that they cannot hear other witnesses' testimony. The court may also do exclude witnesses on its own. But this rule does not authorize excluding: a party who is a natural person; an officer or employee of a party that is not a natural person, after being designated as the party's representative by its attorney; a person whose presence a party shows to be essential to presenting the party's claim or defense; or a person authorized by statute to be present.

ASSIGNMENTS

CASE BRIEF

Read and discuss case 4 - Evidence of other crimes - United States vs. Steven Lane, appellant

ACTIVITY

There are two different situations that arise when a witness cannot immediately recall the facts but is able to do so through the aid of a writing. The rules applying to them in trial are different. Outline how this rule might come into play with an officer's police report.

Evidence of a witness's religious beliefs or opinions is not admissible to attack or support the witness's credibility. What if the victim and defendant are both from the same religious cult? What if a conspiracy occurred within a group of church goers of the same denomination? Explain your answer.

CHAPTER 5 - OPINIONS AND EXPERT TESTIMONY

INTRODUCTION

A person is qualified to testify as an expert if he or she has special knowledge, skill, experience, training or education sufficient to qualify him or her as an expert on the subject to which the testimony relates.

An expert is permitted not only to testify to facts that he or she personally observed but also to state an opinion about certain circumstances. This is allowed because an expert, from experience, research and study, generally has a particular knowledge of the subject of the inquiry and is more capable than a lay person of drawing conclusions from facts and basing an opinion upon them.

An expert witness may state an opinion in response to a hypothetical question. A hypothetical question is one in which the witness is asked to assume that certain facts are true and to give an opinion based on those assumptions. The value of the opinion given by an expert in response to a hypothetical question depends upon the relevance, validity and completeness of the facts he or she was asked to assume.

http://www.jud.ct.gov/ji/criminal/part2/2.5-1.htm

OBJECTIVES

1. Assess what an expert witness may attest to in court

2. Evaluate what qualifies a witness as an expert

3. Compare and contrast a lay witness with an expert witness

KEY TERMS

Expert witness - A person who is permitted to testify at a trial because of special knowledge or proficiency in a particular field that is relevant to the case.

Lay witness - A witness who is not an expert. Lay witnesses may not offer opinions, unless they are based on firsthand knowledge or help to clarify testimony.

Opinion - A belief or judgment short of absolute conviction, certainty, or positive knowledge; it is a conclusion that certain facts are probably true.

Hypothetical - A conceptual imagining of circumstances, that if true, would explain certain facts.

Ultimate issue - An Ultimate issue references a point that is not yet decided and is sufficient in itself or in connection with other points to resolve the entire case. Ultimate issue is sometimes referred to as ultimate question.

OPINION TESTIMONY BY LAY WITNESSES

If a witness is not testifying as an expert, testimony in the form of an opinion is limited to one that is rationally based on the witness's perception; helpful to clearly understanding the witness's testimony or to determining a fact in issue; and not based on scientific, technical, or other specialized knowledge within the scope of an expert witness.

TESTIMONY BY EXPERT WITNESSES

A witness who is qualified as an expert by knowledge, skill, experience, training, or education may testify in the form of an opinion or otherwise if the expert's scientific, technical, or other specialized knowledge will help the trier of fact understand the evidence or determine a fact in issue; the testimony is based on sufficient facts or data; the testimony is the product of reliable principles and methods; and the expert has reliably applied the principles and methods to the facts of the case.

BASIS OF AN EXPERT'S OPINION TESTIMONY

An expert may base an opinion on facts or data in the case that the expert has been made aware of or personally observed. If experts in the particular field would reasonably rely on those kinds of facts or data in forming an opinion on the subject, they need not be admissible for the opinion to be admitted. But if the facts or data would otherwise be inadmissible, the proponent of the opinion may disclose them to the jury only if their probative value in helping the jury evaluate the opinion substantially outweighs their prejudicial effect.

OPINION ON AN ULTIMATE ISSUE

In general, not automatically objectionable

An opinion is not objectionable just because it embraces an ultimate issue.

Exception

In a criminal case, an expert witness must not state an opinion about whether the defendant did or did not have a mental state or condition that constitutes an element of the crime charged or of a defense. Those matters are for the trier of fact alone.

DISCLOSING THE FACTS OR DATA UNDERLYING AN EXPERT'S OPINION

Unless the court orders otherwise, an expert may state an opinion, and give the reasons for it, without first testifying to the underlying facts or data. But the expert may be required to disclose those facts or data on cross-examination.

COURT-APPOINTED EXPERT WITNESSES

Appointment process

On a party's motion or on its own, the court may order the parties to show cause why expert witnesses should not be appointed and may ask the parties to submit nominations. The court may appoint any expert that the parties agree on and any of its own choosing. But the court may only appoint someone who consents to act.

Expert's role

The court must inform the expert of the expert's duties. The court may do so in writing and have a copy filed with the clerk or may do so orally at a conference in which the parties have an opportunity to participate. The expert must advise the parties of any findings the expert makes; may be deposed by any party; may be called to testify by the court or any party; and may be cross-examined by any party, including the party that called the expert.

Compensation

The expert is entitled to a reasonable compensation, as set by the court. The compensation is payable as follows:

- In a criminal case or in a civil case involving just compensation under the Fifth Amendment, from any funds that are provided by law

- In any other civil case, by the parties in the proportion and at the time that the court directs, and the compensation is then charged like other costs

Disclosing the appointment to the jury

The court may authorize disclosure to the jury that the court appointed the expert.

Parties choice of their own exhibits

This rule does not limit a party in calling its own experts.

ASSIGNMENTS

CASE BRIEF

Read and discuss case 5 - Expert witness - United States of America, Plaintiff, v. Mark A. Tindell, Defendant.

ACTIVITY

1. Explain the difference between an expert witness and a lay witness. Identify an example of each.

2. An expert must advise the parties of any findings the expert makes; may be deposed by any party; may be called to testify by the court or any party; and may be cross-examined by any party, including the party that called the expert. Does this guarantee impartiality? What if multiple experts have varying opinions? Find a case in which an expert was used and outline their role in the trial.

CHAPTER 6 - HEARSAY

INTRODUCTION

You may sense that hearsay is defined more by the exceptions rather than the definition. Hearsay is defined simply as evidence of an out of court statement offered to prove the truth of the matter asserted in the statement. The statement can be oral or written.

Hearsay is much more complicated than would be expected. Basically, hearsay rules address someone telling what they heard, rather than what they know from direct observation. Hearsay includes statements made by testifying witnesses.

Those statements are not hearsay only under certain circumstances (if they are inconsistent or if they are consistent and used to rebut a charge of fabrication).

For example, a witness can testify that they saw that the light was red, but they can't say, *"I told someone the other day that I saw that the light was red,"* unless there is a charge that the current testimony is fabricated.

OBJECTIVES

1. Define hearsay from a legal perspective

2. Assess the rules and exceptions to the rules regarding hearsay

KEY TERMS

Statement - A person's oral assertion, written assertion, or nonverbal conduct, if the person intended it as an assertion.

Declarant - The person who made the statement.

Hearsay - A statement outside of the current trial or hearing that a party offers in evidence to prove the truth of the matter asserted in the statement.

STATEMENTS THAT ARE NOT HEARSAY

A statement that meets the following conditions is not hearsay:

A Declarant-Witness's Prior Statement

The declarant testifies and is subject to cross-examination about a prior statement, and the statement is inconsistent with the declarant's testimony and was given under penalty of perjury at a trial, hearing, or other proceeding or in a deposition; or is consistent with the declarant's testimony and is offered to rebut an express or implied charge that the declarant recently fabricated it or acted from a recent improper influence or motive in so testifying; or to rehabilitate the declarant's credibility as a witness when attacked on another ground; or identifies a person as someone the declarant perceived earlier.

An Opposing Party's Statement

The statement is offered against an opposing party and was:

- Made by the party in an individual or representative capacity
- Is one the party manifested that it adopted or believed to be true.
- Made by a person whom the party authorized to make a statement on the subject
- Made by the party's agent or employee on a matter within the scope of that relationship and while it existed
- Made by the party's coconspirator during and in furtherance of the conspiracy.

The statement must be considered but does not by itself establish the declarant's authority under the existence or scope of the relationship, or the existence of the conspiracy, or participation in it the conspiracy.

THE RULE AGAINST HEARSAY

Hearsay is not admissible unless any of the following provides otherwise, a federal statute; the rules of evidence; or other rules prescribed by the Supreme Court.

EXCEPTION - REGARDLESS OF WHETHER THE DECLARANT IS AVAILABLE AS A WITNESS

The following are not excluded by the rule against hearsay, regardless of whether the declarant is available as a witness:

Present Sense Impression

A statement describing or explaining an event or condition, made while or immediately after the declarant perceived it.

Excited Utterance

A statement relating to a startling event or condition, made while the declarant was under the stress of excitement that the event or condition caused.

Then-Existing Mental, Emotional, or Physical Condition

A statement of the declarant's then-existing state of mind (such as motive, intent, or plan) or emotional, sensory, or physical condition (such as mental feeling, pain, or bodily health), but not including a statement of memory or belief to prove the fact remembered or believed unless it relates to the validity or terms of the declarant's will.

Statement Made for Medical Diagnosis or Treatment

A statement that is made for, and is reasonably pertinent to, medical diagnosis or treatment; and describes medical history; past or present symptoms or sensations; their inception; or their general cause.

Recorded Recollection

A record that is on a matter the witness once knew about but now cannot recall well enough to testify fully and accurately; or was made or adopted by the witness when the matter was fresh in the witness's memory; and accurately reflects the witness's knowledge.

If admitted, the record may be read into evidence but may be received as an exhibit only if offered by an adverse party.

Records of a Regularly Conducted Activity (Commonly Referred to as "Business Records")

A record of an act, event, condition, opinion, or diagnosis if: the record was made at or near the time by, or from information transmitted by someone with knowledge; the record was kept in the course of a regularly conducted activity of a business, organization, occupation, or calling, whether or not for profit; making the record was a regular practice of that activity; all these conditions are shown by the testimony of the custodian or another qualified witness, or by a certification consistent with a rule or statute permitting certification; and the opponent does not show that the source of information or the method or circumstances of preparation indicate a lack of trustworthiness.

Absence of a Record of a Regularly Conducted Activity

Evidence that a matter is not included in a record described previously as a record of a regularly conducted activity if the evidence is admitted to prove that the matter did not occur or exist; a record was regularly kept for a matter of that kind; and the opponent does not show that the possible source of the information or other circumstances indicate a lack of trustworthiness.

Public Records

A record or statement of a public office if it sets out:

- The office's activities
- A matter observed while under a legal duty to report, but not including, in a criminal case, a matter observed by law-enforcement personnel; or
- The opponent does not show that the source of information or other circumstances indicate a lack of trustworthiness.

Public Records of Vital Statistics

A record of a birth, death, or marriage, if reported to a public office in accordance with a legal duty

Absence of a Public Record

Testimony that a diligent search failed to disclose a public record or statement if the testimony or certification is admitted to prove that the record or statement does not exist; or a matter did not occur or exist, if a public office regularly kept a record or statement for a matter of that kind

Records of Religious Organizations Concerning Personal or Family History

A statement of birth, legitimacy, ancestry, marriage, divorce, death, relationship by blood or marriage, or similar facts of personal or family history, contained in a regularly kept record of a religious organization.

Certificates of Marriage, Baptism, and Similar Ceremonies

A statement of fact contained in a certificate made by a person who is authorized by a religious organization or by law to perform the act, attesting that the person performed a marriage or similar ceremony or administered a sacrament and purporting to have been issued at the time of the act or within a reasonable time after it.

Family Records

A statement of fact about personal or family history contained in a family record, such as a Bible, genealogy, chart, engraving on a ring, inscription on a portrait, or engraving on an urn or burial marker.

Records of Documents that Affect an Interest in Property.

The record of a document that purports to establish or affect an interest in property if the record is admitted to prove the content of the original recorded document, along with its signing and its delivery by each person who purports to have signed it, the record is kept in a public office, and a statute authorizes recording documents of that kind in that office.

Statements in Documents that Affect an Interest in Property

A statement contained in a document that purports to establish or affect an interest in property if the matter stated was relevant to the document's purpose, unless later dealings with the property are inconsistent with the truth of the statement or the purport of the document.

Statements in Ancient Documents

A statement in a document that is at least 20 years old and whose authenticity is established.

Market Reports and Similar Commercial Publication

Market quotations, lists, directories, or other compilations that are generally relied on by the public or by persons in particular occupations.

Statements in Learned Treatises, Periodicals, or Pamphlets

A statement contained in a treatise, periodical, or pamphlet if the statement is called to the attention of an expert witness on cross-examination or relied on by the expert on direct examination, and the publication is established as a reliable authority by the expert's admission or testimony, by another expert's testimony, or by judicial notice. If admitted, the statement may be read into evidence but not received as an exhibit.

Reputation Concerning Personal or Family History

A reputation among a person's family by blood, adoption, or marriage, or among a person's associates or in the community, concerning the person's birth, adoption, legitimacy, ancestry, marriage, divorce, death, relationship by blood, adoption, or marriage, or similar facts of personal or family history.

Reputation Concerning Boundaries or General History

A reputation in a community, arising before the controversy, concerning boundaries of land in the community or customs that affect the land, or concerning general historical events important to that community, state, or nation.

Reputation Concerning Character

A reputation among a person's associates or in the community concerning the person's character.

Judgment of a Previous Conviction

Evidence of a final judgment of conviction if the judgment was entered after a trial or guilty plea, but not a *nolo contendere* plea, the conviction was for a crime punishable by death or by imprisonment for more than a year, the evidence is admitted to prove any fact essential to the judgment, and when offered by the prosecutor in a criminal case for a purpose other than impeachment, the judgment was against the defendant. The pendency of an appeal may be shown but does not affect admissibility.

Judgments Involving Personal, Family, or General History, or a Boundary

A judgment that is admitted to prove a matter of personal, family, or general history, or boundaries, if the matter was essential to the judgment, and could be proved by evidence of reputation.

EXCEPTION - WHEN THE DECLARANT IS UNAVAILABLE AS A WITNESS

CRITERIA FOR BEING UNAVAILABLE

A declarant is considered to be unavailable as a witness if the declarant:

- Is exempted from testifying about the subject matter of the declarant's statement because the court rules that a privilege applies;
- Refuses to testify about the subject matter despite a court order to do so;
- Testifies to not remembering the subject matter;
- Cannot be present or testify at the trial or hearing because of death or a then-existing infirmity, physical illness, or mental illness; or
- Is absent from the trial or hearing and the statement's proponent has not been able, by process or other reasonable means, to procure the declarant's attendance or testimony.

These do not apply if the statement's proponent procured or wrongfully caused the declarant's unavailability as a witness to prevent the declarant from attending or testifying.

THE EXCEPTIONS

The following are not excluded by the rule against hearsay if the declarant is unavailable as a witness:

Former Testimony.

Testimony that was given as a witness at a trial, hearing, or lawful deposition, whether given during the current proceeding or a different one, and is now offered against a party who had, or in a civil case, whose predecessor in interest had, an opportunity and similar motive to develop it by direct, cross, or redirect examination.

Statement Under the Belief of Imminent Death

In a prosecution for homicide or in a civil case, a statement that the declarant, while believing the declarant's death to be imminent, made about its cause or circumstances. This is sometimes called a "dying declaration."

Statement Against Interest

A statement that a reasonable person in the declarant's position would have made only if the person believed it to be true because, when made, it was so contrary to the declarant's proprietary or pecuniary interest or had so great a tendency to invalidate the declarant's claim against someone else or to expose the declarant to civil or criminal liability, and is supported by corroborating circumstances that clearly indicate its trustworthiness, if it is offered in a criminal case as one that tends to expose the declarant to criminal liability.

Statement of Personal or Family History

A statement about the declarant's own birth, adoption, legitimacy, ancestry, marriage, divorce, relationship by blood, adoption, or marriage, or similar facts of personal or family history, even though the declarant had no way of acquiring personal knowledge about that fact, or another person concerning any of these facts, as well as death, if the declarant was related to the person by blood, adoption, or marriage or was so intimately associated with the person's family that the declarant's information is likely to be accurate.

Statement Offered Against a Party That Wrongfully Caused the Declarant's Unavailability

A statement offered against a party that wrongfully caused, or acquiesced in wrongfully causing, the declarant's unavailability as a witness, and did so intending that result.

HEARSAY WITHIN HEARSAY

Hearsay within hearsay is not excluded by the rule against hearsay if each part of the combined statements conforms with an exception to the rule.

Attacking and Supporting the Declarant's Credibility

When a hearsay statement has been admitted in evidence, the declarant's credibility may be attacked, and then supported, by any evidence that would be admissible for those purposes if the declarant had testified as a witness. The court may admit evidence of the declarant's inconsistent statement or conduct, regardless of when it occurred or whether the declarant had an opportunity to explain or deny it. If the party against whom the statement was admitted calls the declarant as a witness, the party may examine the declarant on the statement as if on cross-examination.

Residual Exception

Under the following circumstances, a hearsay statement is not excluded by the rule against hearsay even if the statement is not specifically covered by a hearsay exception:

- The statement has equivalent circumstantial guarantees of trustworthiness;

- It is offered as evidence of a material fact;

- It is more probative on the point for which it is offered than any other evidence that the proponent can obtain through reasonable efforts; and

- Admitting it will best serve the purposes of these rules and the interests of justice.

The statement is admissible only if, before the trial or hearing, the proponent gives an adverse party reasonable notice of the intent to offer the statement and its particulars, including the declarant's name and address, so that the party has a fair opportunity to meet it.

ASSIGNMENTS

CASE BRIEF

Read and discuss case 6 - Character - United States of America v. Arthur Michael Kinsella, defendant

ACTIVITY

1. There are numerous exceptions to the hearsay rule. Explain the dying declaration example. Identify a case in which a dying declaration was used.

2. A witness can be challenged using former testimony. Identify and example of this.

CHAPTER 7 - AUTHENTICATION AND IDENTIFICATION

INTRODUCTION

To satisfy the requirement of authenticating or identifying an item of evidence, the proponent must produce evidence sufficient to support a finding that the item is what the proponent claims it is.

OBJECTIVES

1. Explore the rules for evidence to be deemed authentic

KEY TERMS

Self-authenticating - Authorship or origin is conclusively or unquestionably established on its face

Public document - Document such as court records, deeds, and public registers authenticated by a public officer and made available for public reference and use

THE REQUIREMENTS OF AUTHENTICITY

The following are examples only, not a complete list, of evidence that satisfies the requirement of authenticity:

Testimony of a Witness with Knowledge

Testimony that an item is what it is claimed to be.

Non-expert Opinion About Handwriting

A non-expert's opinion that handwriting is genuine, based on a familiarity with it that was not acquired for the current litigation.

Comparison by an Expert Witness or the Trier of Fact

A comparison with an authenticated specimen by an expert witness or the trier of fact.

Distinctive Characteristics and the Like

The appearance, contents, substance, internal patterns, or other distinctive characteristics of the item, taken together with all the circumstances.

Opinion About a Voice

An opinion identifying a person's voice, whether heard firsthand or through mechanical or electronic transmission or recording, based on hearing the voice at any time under circumstances that connect it with the alleged speaker.

Evidence About a Telephone Conversation

For a telephone conversation, evidence that a call was made to the number assigned at the time to a particular person, if circumstances, including self-identification, show that the person answering was the one called, or a particular business, if the call was made to a business and the call related to business reasonably transacted over the telephone.

Evidence About Public Records

Evidence that a document was recorded or filed in a public office as authorized by law, or a purported public record or statement is from the office where items of this kind are kept.

Evidence About Ancient Documents or Data Compilations

For a document or data compilation, evidence that it is in a condition that creates no suspicion about its authenticity, was in a place where, if authentic, it would likely be, and is at least 20 years old when offered.

Evidence About a Process or System

Evidence describing a process or system and showing that it produces an accurate result.

Methods Provided by a Statute or Rule

Any method of authentication or identification allowed by a federal statute or a rule prescribed by the Supreme Court.

EVIDENCE THAT IS SELF-AUTHENTICATING

The following items of evidence are self-authenticating; they require no extrinsic evidence of authenticity in order to be admitted:

Domestic Public Documents that are Sealed and Signed

A document that bears a seal purporting to be that of the United States; any state, district, commonwealth, territory, or insular possession of the United States; the former Panama Canal Zone; the Trust Territory of the Pacific Islands; a political subdivision of any of these entities; or a department, agency, or officer of any entity named above, and a signature purporting to be an execution or attestation.

Domestic Public Documents that are not Sealed but are Signed and Certified

A document that bears no seal if it bears the signature of an officer or employee of an official entity and another public officer who has a seal and official duties within that same entity certifies under seal, or its equivalent, that the signer has the official capacity and that the signature is genuine.

Foreign Public Documents

A document that purports to be signed or attested by a person who is authorized by a foreign country's law to do so. The document must be accompanied by a final certification that certifies the genuineness of the signature and official position of the signer or attester, or of any foreign official whose certificate of genuineness relates to the signature or attestation or is in a chain of certificates of genuineness relating to the signature or attestation. The certification may be made by a secretary of a United States embassy or legation; by a consul general, vice consul, or consular agent of the United States; or by a diplomatic or consular official of the foreign country assigned or accredited to the United States. If all parties have been given a reasonable opportunity to investigate the document's authenticity and accuracy, the court may, for good cause, either order that it be treated as presumptively authentic without final certification or allow it to be evidenced by an attested summary with or without final certification.

Certified Copies of Public Records

A copy of an official record, or a copy of a document that was recorded or filed in a public office as authorized by law, if the copy is certified as correct by the custodian or another person authorized to make the certification, or a certificate that complies with a federal statute, or a rule prescribed by the Supreme Court.

Official Publications

A book, pamphlet, or other publication purporting to be issued by a public authority.

Newspapers and Periodicals

Printed material purporting to be a newspaper or periodical.

Trade Inscriptions and the Like

An inscription, sign, tag, or label purporting to have been affixed in the course of business and indicating origin, ownership, or control.

Acknowledged Documents

A document accompanied by a certificate of acknowledgment that is lawfully executed by a notary public or another officer who is authorized to take acknowledgments.

Commercial Paper and Related Documents

Commercial paper, a signature on it, and related documents, to the extent allowed by general commercial law.

Presumptions Under a Federal Statute

A signature, document, or anything else that a federal statute declares to be presumptively or *prima facie* genuine or authentic.

Certified Domestic Records of a Regularly Conducted Activity

The original or a copy of a domestic record as shown by a certification of the custodian or another qualified person that complies with a federal statute or a rule prescribed by the Supreme Court. Before the trial or hearing, the proponent must give an adverse party reasonable written notice of the intent to offer the record and must make the record and certification available for inspection, so that the party has a fair opportunity to challenge them.

Certified Foreign Records of a Regularly Conducted Activity

In a civil case, the original or a copy of a foreign record modified as follows: the certification, rather than complying with a federal statute or Supreme Court rule, must be signed in a manner that, if falsely made, would subject the maker to a criminal penalty in the country where the certification is signed.

SUBSCRIBING WITNESS'S TESTIMONY

A subscribing witness's testimony is necessary to authenticate a writing only if required by the law of the jurisdiction that governs its validity.

ASSIGNMENTS

CASE BRIEF

Read and discuss case 7 - Business records - United States District Court for the District of Columbia - Memorandum opinion

ACTIVITY

1. An opinion identifying a person's voice, whether heard firsthand or through mechanical or electronic transmission or recording, based on hearing the voice at any time under circumstances that connect it with the alleged speaker is a form of authentication. Can you identify any concerns about that method? Has this been used in criminal cases before?

2. Included in self-certifying examples, a copy of an official record, or a copy of a document that was recorded or filed in a public office as authorized by law, if the copy is certified as correct by the custodian or another person authorized to make the certification. Identify an example in which this was used and how it was used.

CHAPTER 8 - CONTENTS OF WRITINGS, RECORDINGS, AND PHOTOGRAPHS

INTRODUCTION

The best evidence rule provides that, where the contents of a document are to be proved, the party must either produce the original or show a sufficient excuse for its non-production. The rule is a doctrine of evidentiary preference principally aimed, not at securing a writing at all hazards and in every instance, but at securing the best obtainable evidence of its contents. Thus, where the original has been lost, destroyed, or is otherwise unavailable, its production may be excused and other evidence of its contents will be admissible, provided that certain findings are made. [Quotation and citations omitted; emphasis omitted]

OBJECTIVES

1. Assess the rules regarding admissibility of written, recorded, and photographic evidence

2. Compare and contrast the requirements of admissibility if the original item has been destroyed

KEY TERMS

Writing - Consists of letters, words, numbers, or their equivalent set down in any form.

Recording - Consists of letters, words, numbers, or their equivalent recorded in any manner.

Photograph - Means a photographic image or its equivalent stored in any form.

Original - An original of a writing or recording means the writing or recording itself or any counterpart intended to have the same effect by the person who executed or issued it. For electronically stored information, "original" means any printout, or other output readable by sight, if it accurately reflects the information. An "original" of a photograph includes the negative or a print from it.

Duplicate - Means a counterpart produced by a mechanical, photographic, chemical, electronic, or other equivalent process or technique that accurately reproduces the original.

REQUIREMENT OF THE ORIGINAL

An original writing, recording, or photograph is required to prove its content unless these rules or a federal statute provides otherwise.

ADMISSIBILITY OF DUPLICATES

A duplicate is admissible to the same extent as the original unless a genuine question is raised about the original's authenticity or the circumstances make it unfair to admit the duplicate.

ADMISSIBILITY OF OTHER EVIDENCE OF CONTENT

An original is not required and other evidence of the content of a writing, recording, or photograph is admissible if all the originals are lost or destroyed, and not by the proponent acting in bad faith, an original cannot be obtained by any available judicial process, the party against whom the original would be offered had control of the original, was at that time put on notice, by pleadings or otherwise, that the original would be a subject of proof at the trial or hearing; and fails to produce it at the trial or hearing, or the writing, recording, or photograph is not closely related to a controlling issue.

COPIES OF PUBLIC RECORDS TO PROVE CONTENT

The proponent may use a copy to prove the content of an official record, or of a document that was recorded or filed in a public office as authorized by law, if these conditions are met: the record or document is otherwise admissible; and the copy is certified as correct, or is testified to be correct by a witness who has compared it with the original. If no such copy can be obtained by reasonable diligence, then the proponent may use other evidence to prove the content.

SUMMARIES TO PROVE CONTENT

The proponent may use a summary, chart, or calculation to prove the content of voluminous writings, recordings, or photographs that cannot be conveniently examined in court. The proponent must make the originals or duplicates available for examination or copying, or both, by other parties at a reasonable time and place. And the court may order the proponent to produce them in court.

TESTIMONY OR STATEMENT OF A PARTY TO PROVE CONTENT

The proponent may prove the content of a writing, recording, or photograph by the testimony, deposition, or written statement of the party against whom the evidence is offered. The proponent need not account for the original.

FUNCTIONS OF THE COURT AND JURY

Ordinarily, the court determines whether the proponent has fulfilled the factual conditions for admitting other evidence of the content of a writing, recording, or photograph. But in a jury trial, the jury determines any issue about whether an asserted writing, recording, or photograph ever existed, another one produced at the trial or hearing is the original, or other evidence of content accurately reflects the content.

ASSIGNMENTS

CASE BRIEF

Read and discuss Case 8 - Hearsay - Supreme Court of the United States Syllabus - Ohio v Clark Certiorari to the Supreme Court of Ohio

ACTIVITY

1. If an original document has been destroyed, is it possible to submit a duplicate as evidence? What standards must be met? Identify an example in which a duplicate was admitted as evidence

2. Included in self-certifying examples, a copy of an official record, or a copy of a document that was recorded or filed in a public office as authorized by law, if the copy is certified as correct by the custodian or another person authorized to make the certification. Identify an example in which this was used and how it was used.

THE BILL OF RIGHTS

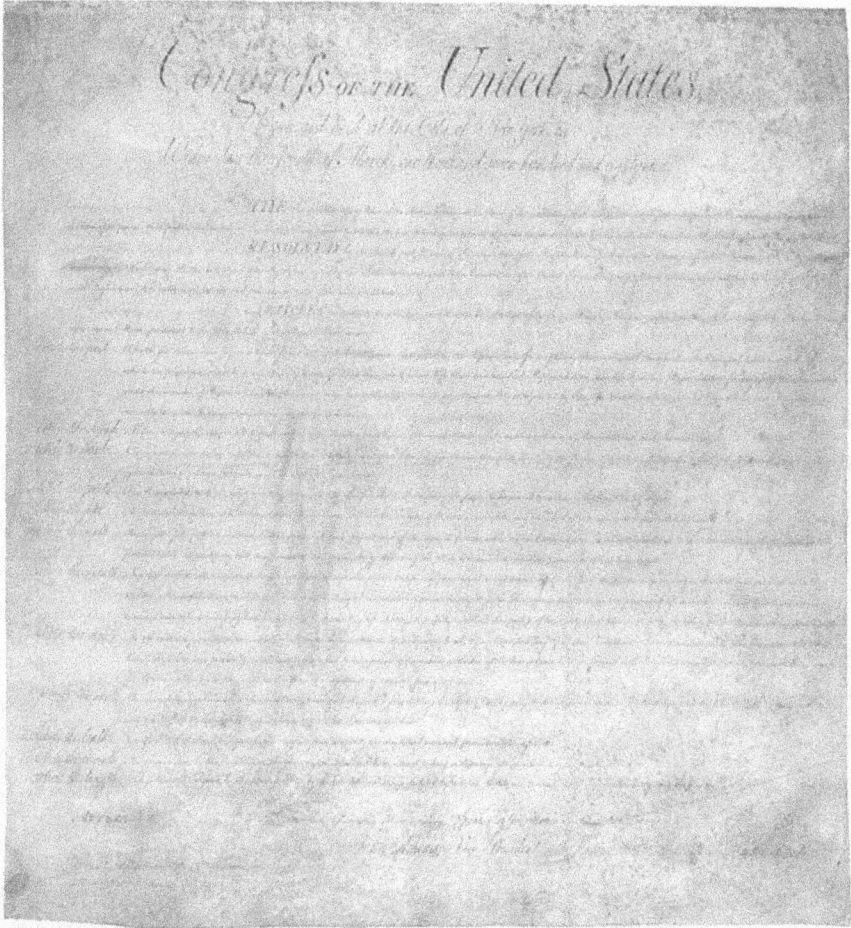

AMENDMENT I

Congress shall make no law respecting an establishment of religion, or prohibiting the free exercise thereof; or abridging the freedom of speech, or of the press; or the right of the people peaceably to assemble, and to petition the Government for a redress of grievances.

Key points:

- *The government cannot establish a national religion*
- *The government cannot prohibit religious practices*
- *The government cannot abridge free speech*
- *The government cannot abridge the press*
- *The government cannot prohibit peaceful assembly*
- *The people have the right to petition for redress of grievances.*

AMENDMENT II

A well regulated Militia, being necessary to the security of a free State, the right of the people to keep and bear Arms, shall not be infringed.

> *Key point:*
> - *The people have the right to keep and bear arms*

AMENDMENT III

No Soldier shall, in time of peace be quartered in any house, without the consent of the Owner, nor in time of war, but in a manner to be prescribed by law.

> *Key point:*
> - *The government cannot require homeowners to house soldiers*

AMENDMENT IV

The right of the people to be secure in their persons, houses, papers, and effects, against unreasonable searches and seizures, shall not be violated, and no Warrants shall issue, but upon probable cause, supported by Oath or affirmation, and particularly describing the place to be searched, and the persons or things to be seized.

> *Key points:*

> – *The government cannot search or seize your person, house, papers, or effects without a warrant that is based on probably cause and sworn oath*
> – *Warrants that are issued must 'particularly' describe the place to be searched and any person or thing to be seized*

AMENDMENT V

No person shall be held to answer for a capital, or otherwise infamous crime, unless on a presentment or indictment of a Grand Jury, except in cases arising in the land or naval forces, or in the Militia, when in actual service in time of War or public danger; nor shall any person be subject for the same offence to be twice put in jeopardy of life or limb; nor shall be compelled in any criminal case to be a witness against himself, nor be deprived of life, liberty, or property, without due process of law; nor shall private property be taken for public use, without just compensation.

> *Key points:*
> – *No person can be charged with a serious crime unless there is an indictment by a grand jury (exception time of war or emergency)*
> – *No one can be charged twice for the same crime*
> – *No one is required to testify against themselves*
> – *No one can be deprived of life, liberty, or property without due process*
> – *The owner of any property taken for public use must receive just compensation*

AMENDMENT VI

In all criminal prosecutions, the accused shall enjoy the right to a speedy and public trial, by an impartial jury of the State and district wherein the crime shall have been committed, which district shall have been previously ascertained by law, and to be informed of the nature and cause of the accusation; to be confronted with the witnesses against him; to have compulsory process for obtaining witnesses in his favor, and to have the Assistance of Counsel for his defense.

> *Key Points:*
>
> — *Persons accused of a crime shall have a speedy trial*
>
> — *Persons accused of a crime shall have a public trial by an impartial jury*
>
> — *Trials will be held in the area where the crime was committed*
>
> — *Persons accused of a crime have a right to be told the nature and cause of the accusation*
>
> — *Persons accused of a crime have the right to confront witnesses who are used against them*
>
> — *Persons accused of a crime have the right to a process to obtain witnesses who may testify in their favor*
>
> — *Persons accused of a crime have the right to counsel*

AMENDMENT VII

In Suits at common law, where the value in controversy shall exceed twenty dollars, the right of trial by jury shall be preserved, and no fact tried by a jury, shall be otherwise re-examined in any Court of the United States, than *(sic)* according to the rules of the common law.

> *Key points:*
> — *The Right and the Characteristics of the Civil Jury*

AMENDMENT VIII

Excessive bail shall not be required, nor excessive fines imposed, nor cruel and unusual punishments inflicted.

> *Key points:*
> - *Excessive bail shall not be required*
> - *Excessive fines shall not be imposed*
> - *Cruel and unusual punishment shall not be inflicted*

AMENDMENT IX

The enumeration in the Constitution, of certain rights, shall not be construed to deny or disparage others retained by the people.

> *Key point:*
> - *Rights outlined in the Constitution cannot be used to deny other rights retained by the people.*

AMENDMENT X

The powers not delegated to the United States by the Constitution, nor prohibited by it to the States, are reserved to the States respectively, or to the people.

> *Key point:*
> - *Any powers the constitution does not delegate to the federal government, or powers the constitution prohibits the states from having, are reserved to the states, or to the people.*

CASES

The following eight cases address the rules of evidence issues discussed in the textbook.

CASE 1 - PRIVILEGE

CASE BRIEF - IN THE UNITED STATES DISTRICT COURT FOR THE SOUTHERN DISTRICT OF ALABAMA SOUTHERN DIVISION

UNITED STATES OF AMERICA vs.

LEROY WATERS, et al. Defendants.

Criminal Action No. 11-00012-KD ORDER

This action is before the Court on the motion for partial suppression and a taint hearing as to the Government's invasion of privilege filed by defendant Chris Vernon (doc. 159), defendant Jeff Vernon's joinder in the motion (doc. 181), the Government's response (doc. 201), Chris Vernon's memorandum in further support of the motion (doc. 234), Jeff Vernon's joinder in the memorandum (doc. 236), and the United States' memorandum in further support of its response (doc. 315). A hearing was held on December 13, 2011. Defendant Chris Vernon and his defense counsel Jackson R. Sharman III, defendant Jeff Vernon and his defense counsel James R. Sturdivant, and counsel for the United States, Assistant United States Attorney Adam W. Overstreet participated in the hearing.

The defendants seek to suppress the government's use of allegedly ill-gotten privileged material. Specifically, the defendants request that the court order:

> 1) the government to cease review of the material until appropriate measures are taken to protect privileged material;
>
> 2) the government to segregate and return all potentially privileged material;
>
> 3) the implementation of a schedule for a privilege log and appoint a special master to hear objections to same which ultimately requires the government to destroy any privileged material in its possession;
>
> 4) suppression of all privileged materials seized from Medfusion;

> 5) and order that defendants be allowed to use privileged material without generally waiving the attorney-client privilege.

The defendants have spent most of their brief explaining the government's deficiencies in the handling of electronically stored information (ESI). Specifically, the defendants outline in great detail what the government should have done when they seized the records of Medfusion in order to avoid coming in contact with attorney-client privileged information. Apparently, the government seized the ESI records and then initially searched looking for relevant information without concern for finding privileged information.

The defendants initially identified eleven (11) emails in the government's possession that appear to contain privileged information. In a "privilege log", the defendants contend that they have identified "over four-hundred pages spread across sixty-six documents that either contain privileged material or indicate affirmatively that the Government processed privileged material." The defendants further contend that as of December 9, 2011 "the extent of the Government's intrusion is presently unknown.".

The government responds by arguing:

1) that the defendants' objection to the government's possession of privileged material is untimely, thus they have waived the attorney-client privilege;

2) that only a "negligible" amount of privileged information is at issue;

3) that the defendants have no Sixth Amendment right for the government not to intrude on the attorney-client privilege during a search and seizure; and

4) even if the defendants did have such a right, the defendants have failed to show prejudice whereas to warrant the sanctions requested. The government also suggests a procedure for prospective review of potential attorney-client material which would include review by an FBI "filter paralegal" and a "filter AUSA".

The court's review of the dispute regarding how the materials will be processed is moot, in that the case is now set for trial and presumably the investigatory stage is mostly complete. Thus, the only remaining issue is whether the government has possession of any privileged information and whether they have made any use of this information that is detrimental to the defendants.

Waiver

In United States v. Ary, 518 F. 3d 775 (10th Cir. 2008), the Court of Appeals for the Tenth Circuit identified three factors which courts have considered when deciding waiver of privilege as to material involuntarily disclosed:

1) "the specificity with which the defendant identifies the material;

2) the expediency by which the defendant informs the government that it seized protected material; and

3) the expediency by which the defendant seeks judicial action to enforce the protection."

The circuit court in Ary also stated that the "party asserting the . . . attorney- client privilege must pursue all reasonable means to preserve the confidentiality of the material."

The court finds that the defendants did not waive their attorney-client privilege as to the documents seized by waiting to assert such privilege until after they were indicted instead of when the search occurred. While there is reason to believe that the defendants may have known that ESI was seized, no inventory of exactly what ESI was seized was provided to the defendants until arraignment, and even now there is a dispute whether that inventory is complete.

Moreover, when defendants became aware that the hard drives and email server had been imaged, they promptly communicated with the government and began to identify certain documents allegedly privileged, i.e., the eleven emails, and ultimately filed the instant motion.

Sixth Amendment Violation

The court does not find that a Sixth Amendment violation has occurred; thus, sanctions are not warranted. A constitutional violation occurs only when the government intentionally intrudes into an attorney-client relationship and therein obtains confidential information regarding the defense of the allegations and then uses that information to the defendants' detriment. "Because intrusions into the attorney-client relationship are not per se unconstitutional, establishing a Sixth Amendment violation requires some showing of prejudice in terms of injury to the defendant or benefit to the State." (where there is no demonstrable prejudice to the defendant or a substantial threat of same, dismissing the indictment as a sanction for government intrusion into the attorney- client relationship is not appropriate); (defendants bear the burden of establishing that privileged material was given to the prosecution team and that defendants have been prejudiced).

First, the government's intrusion into the attorney-client relationship may have been negligent, or even grossly so, but there is no evidence that it was intentional. There is no evidence that the government was on actual notice that the ESI would contain privileged information, although it would appear that the government should have anticipated such and set up appropriate safeguards. Such safeguards are articulated in case law as well as the Department of Justice policy manual in order to avoid the current situation. With that said, the fact that the government did not act in accordance with their own policy is not a basis for finding a Sixth Amendment violation. As previously stated, the intrusion must be intentional. There is no evidence that the government set out to discover privileged information through the search.

Second, because the trial has not been held, defendants have not shown that any privileged information has been used to their detriment at trial. Thus, defendants must show that they have sustained "substantial detriment" in "some other way". This they have not done except to assert that the prosecution team is now presumed to be tainted by the alleged access to privileged information. However, "so long as no evidence stemming from the breach of the privilege is introduced at trial, no prejudice results". Additionally, there is no evidence that obtaining the allegedly confidential information in the ESI resulted in a "benefit to the prosecution." Moreover, the government appears to have put in place protections after the existence of the potentially privileged communications in the ESI was brought to its attention by the defendants.

Privilege Assertion

Regardless of whether a Sixth Amendment violation has been established, the defendants may assert the attorney-client privilege to prevent the government from using any information gained from the privileged documents. Defendants have asserted the privilege. Thus, the issue to be resolved is whether the government has privileged information which should be suppressed.

The attorney-client privilege is designed "to encourage full and frank communication between attorneys and their clients and thereby promote broader public interests in the observance of law and administration of justice." Thus, the privilege protects disclosures that a client makes to his or its attorney, in confidence, for the purpose of securing legal advice or assistance. The privilege also extends to legal advice communicated by an attorney to his client, (The privilege exists to protect not only the giving of professional advice to those who can act on it but also the giving of information to the lawyer to enable him to give sound and informed advice.").

Communications between and attorney and his client for a purpose other than seeking or providing legal advice is not within the privilege.

The burdens of proving the existence of an attorney-client relationship and the confidentiality of communications rest with the party invoking the privilege.

A communication is protected by the attorney-client privilege and protected from Government intrusion if it is "(1) intended to remain confidential and (2) under the circumstances was reasonably expected and understood to be confidential." ("In order to show that communications made to an attorney are within the privilege, it must be shown that the communication was made to him confidentially, in his professional capacity, for the purpose of securing legal advice or assistance."

Communications made in furtherance of an ongoing or intended crime or fraud are not protected by the attorney-client privilege. Courts in the Eleventh Circuit employ a two- part test to examine the applicability of the crime-fraud exception. First, there must be a prima facie showing that (a) the client was engaged in criminal or fraudulent conduct when he sought the advice of counsel; (b) the client was planning such conduct when he sought the advice of counsel; or (c) the client committed a crime or fraud subsequent to receiving the benefit of counsel's advice.

Second, there must be a showing that the attorney's assistance was obtained in furtherance of the criminal or fraudulent activity or was closely related to it. The requirement that the attorney's legal advice must be related to the client's criminal or fraudulent conduct "should not be interpreted restrictively."

With respect to the two-part test articulated in Schroeder, the Eleventh Circuit has held that "[t]he first prong is satisfied by a showing of evidence that, if believed by a trier of fact, would establish the elements of some violation that was ongoing or about to be committed," while the second prong is satisfied "by a showing that the communication is related to the criminal or fraudulent activity established under the first prong." For the exception to apply, an attorney need not be aware that his client intends for the advice to be used to effect a crime or fraud; the client's purpose, not the attorney's awareness thereof, is determinative.

On December 22, 2011, the court held a brief telephone conference with James R. Sturdivant, defense counsel for Jeff Vernon; Jackson Sharman, defense counsel for Chris Vernon and Assistant United States Attorney Steven Butler participating on behalf of the filter team established by the government. At the conference, the court explained that as to the 66 documents submitted by the defendants and 407 pages submitted by the government, it appeared there was no overlap. In other words, it appears that the parties derived their documents from two different sources. The participants then agreed that they would exchange documents with only the filter team to have possession of defendants' 66 documents, resolve whether these documents and other documents not before the court are protected by the attorney-client privilege, and inform the court promptly whether further assistance from the court is necessary on this issue.

DONE and **ORDERED** this the 22nd day of December 2011.

/s/ Kristi K. DuBose
KRISTI K. DuBOSE
UNITED STATES DISTRICT JUDGE

CASE 2 - HEARSAY

Ohio v. Roberts.

No. 78-756.
448 U.S. 56 (1980) Supreme Court of United States. Argued November 26, 1979. Decided June 25, 1980.

CERTIORARI TO THE SUPREME COURT OF OHIO.

John E. Shoop argued the cause and filed a brief for petitioner. Marvin R. Plasco argued the cause and filed a brief for respondent

MR. JUSTICE BLACKMUN delivered the opinion of the Court.

This case presents issues concerning the constitutional propriety of the introduction in evidence of the preliminary hearing testimony of a witness not produced at the defendant's subsequent state criminal trial.

I

Local police arrested respondent, Herschel Roberts, on January 7, 1975, in Lake County, Ohio. Roberts was charged with forgery of a check in the name of Bernard Isaacs, and with possession of stolen credit cards belonging to Isaacs and his wife Amy.

A preliminary hearing was held in Municipal Court on January 10. The prosecution called several witnesses, including Mr. Isaacs. Respondent's appointed counsel had seen the Isaacs' daughter, Anita, in the courthouse hallway, and called her as the defense's only witness.

Anita Isaacs testified that she knew respondent, and that she had permitted him to use her apartment for several days while she was away. Defense counsel questioned Anita at some length and attempted to elicit from her an admission that she had given respondent checks and the credit cards without informing him that she did not have permission to use them. Anita, however, denied this. Respondent's attorney did not ask to have the witness declared hostile and did not request permission to place her on cross-examination. The prosecutor did not question Anita.

A county grand jury subsequently indicted respondent for forgery, for receiving stolen property (including the credit cards), and for possession of heroin. The attorney who represented respondent at the preliminary hearing withdrew upon [*59] becoming a Municipal Court Judge, and new counsel was appointed for Roberts.

Between November 1975 and March 1976, five subpoenas for four different trial dates were issued to Anita at her parents' Ohio residence. The last three carried a written instruction that Anita should "call before appearing." She was not at the residence when these were executed. She did not telephone and she did not appear at trial.

1

In March 1976, the case went to trial before a jury in the Court of Common Pleas. Respondent took the stand and testified that Anita Isaacs had given him her parents' checkbook and credit cards with the understanding that he could use them. Relying on Ohio Rev. Code which permits the use of preliminary examination testimony of a witness who "cannot for any reason be produced at the trial," the State, on rebuttal, offered the transcript of Anita's testimony.

Asserting a violation of the Confrontation Clause the defense objected to the use of the transcript. The trial court conducted a voir dire hearing as to its admissibility. Amy Isaacs, the sole witness at voir dire, was questioned by both the prosecutor and defense counsel concerning her daughter's whereabouts. Anita, according to her mother, left home for Tucson, Ariz., soon after the preliminary hearing. About a year before the trial, a San Francisco social worker was in communication with the Isaacs about a welfare application Anita had filed there. Through the social worker, the Isaacs reached their daughter once by telephone. Since then, however, Anita had called her parents only one other time and had not been in touch with her two sisters. When Anita called, some seven or eight months before trial, she told her parents that she "was traveling" outside Ohio, but did not reveal the place from which she called. Mrs. Isaacs stated that she knew of no way to reach Anita in case of an emergency. Nor did she "know of anybody who knows where she is. The trial court admitted the transcript into evidence. Respondent was convicted on all counts.

The Court of Appeals of Ohio reversed. After reviewing the voir dire, that court concluded that the prosecution had failed to make a showing of a "good-faith effort" to secure the absent witness' attendance, as required by Barber v. Page, 390 U. S. 719, 722-725 (1968). The court noted that "we have no witness from the prosecution to testify . . . that no one on behalf of the State could determine Anita's whereabouts, [or] that anyone had exhausted contact with the San Francisco social worker."

Unavailability would have been established, the court said, "[h]ad the State demonstrated that its subpoenas were never actually served on the witness and that they were unable to make contact in any way with the witness. . . . Until the Isaacs' voir dire, requested by the defense, the State had done nothing, absolutely nothing, to show the Court that Anita would be absent because of unavailability, and they showed no effort having been made to seek out her whereabouts for purpose of trial."

The Supreme Court of Ohio, by a 4-3 vote, affirmed, but did so on other grounds. It first held that the Court of Appeals had erred in concluding that Anita was not unavailable. Barber v. Page was distinguished as a case in which "the government knew where [*61] the absent witness was," whereas Anita's "whereabouts were entirely unknown."

"[T]he trial judge could reasonably have concluded from Mrs. Isaacs' voir dire testimony that due diligence could not have procured the attendance of Anita Isaacs"; he "could reasonably infer that Anita had left San Francisco"; and he "could properly hold that the witness was unavailable to testify in person."

The court, nonetheless, held that the transcript was inadmissible. Reasoning that normally there is little incentive to cross-examine a witness at a preliminary hearing, where the "ultimate issue" is only probable cause, and citing the dissenting opinion in California v. Green, 399 U. S. 149, 189 (1970), the court held that the mere opportunity to cross- examine at a preliminary hearing did not afford constitutional confrontation for purposes of trial.

The court distinguished Green, where this Court had ruled admissible the preliminary hearing testimony of a declarant who was present at trial but claimed forgetfulness. The Ohio court perceived a "dictum" in Green that suggested that the mere opportunity to cross-examine renders preliminary hearing testimony admissible. But the court concluded that Green "goes no further than to suggest that cross- examination actually conducted at preliminary hearing may afford adequate confrontation for purposes of a later trial." Since Anita had not been cross-examined at the preliminary hearing and was absent at trial, the introduction of the transcript of her testimony was held to have violated respondent's confrontation right. The three dissenting justices would have ruled that "'the test is the opportunity for full and complete cross-examination rather than the use which is made of that opportunity'"

We granted certiorari to consider these important issues under the Confrontation Clause.

II A

The Court here is called upon to consider once again the relationship between the Confrontation Clause and the hearsay rule with its many exceptions. The basic rule against hearsay, of course, is riddled with exceptions developed over three centuries. These exceptions vary among jurisdictions as to number, nature, and detail. But every set of exceptions seems to fit an apt description offered more than 40 years ago: "an old-fashioned crazy quilt made of patches cut from a group of paintings by cubists, futurists and surrealists." Morgan & Maguire, Looking Backward and Forward at Evidence, 50 Harv. L. Rev. 909, 921 (1937).

The Sixth Amendment's Confrontation Clause, made applicable to the States through the Fourteenth Amendment, provides: "In all criminal prosecutions, the accused shall enjoy the right . . . to be confronted with the witnesses against him." If one were to read this language literally, it would require, on objection, the exclusion of any statement made by a declarant not present at trial. ("There could be nothing more directly contrary to the letter of the provision in question than the admission of dying declarations"). But, if thus applied, the Clause would abrogate virtually every hearsay exception, a result long rejected as unintended and too extreme.

The historical evidence leaves little doubt, however, that the Clause was intended to exclude some hearsay. Moreover, underlying policies support the same conclusion. The Court has emphasized that the Confrontation Clause reflects a preference for face-to-face confrontation at trial, and that "a primary interest secured by [the provision] is the right of cross-examination."

In short, the Clause envisions "a personal examination and cross-examination of the witness in which the accused has an opportunity, not only of testing the recollection and sifting the conscience of the witness, but of compelling him to stand face to face with the jury in order that they may look at him, and judge by his demeanor upon the stand and the manner in which he gives his testimony whether he is worthy of belief."

These means of testing accuracy are so important that the absence of proper confrontation at trial "calls into question the ultimate `integrity of the fact-finding process.'"

The Court, however, has recognized that competing interests, if "closely examined," may warrant dispensing with confrontation at trial. See *Mattox* v. *United States*, 156 U. S., at 243 ("general rules of law of this kind, however beneficent in their operation and valuable to the accused, must occasionally give way to considerations of public policy and the necessities of the case"). Significantly, every jurisdiction has a strong interest in effective law enforcement, and in the development and precise formulation of the rules of evidence applicable in criminal proceedings.

This Court, in a series of cases, has sought to accommodate these competing interests. True to the common-law tradition, the process has been gradual, building on past decisions, drawing on new experience, and responding to changing conditions. The Court has not sought to "map out a theory of the Confrontation Clause that would determine the validity of all . . . hearsay `exceptions.'" 162. But a general approach to the problem is discernible.

B

The Confrontation Clause operates in two separate ways to restrict the range of admissible hearsay. First, in conformance with the Framers' preference for face-to-face accusation, the Sixth Amendment establishes a rule of necessity. In the usual case (including cases where prior cross-examination has occurred), the prosecution must either produce, or demonstrate the unavailability of, the declarant whose statement it wishes to use against the defendant.

The second aspect operates once a witness is shown to be unavailable. Reflecting its underlying purpose to augment accuracy in the factfinding process by ensuring the defendant an effective means to test adverse evidence, the Clause countenances only hearsay marked with such trustworthiness that "there is no material departure from the reason of the general rule."

"The focus of the Court's concern has been to insure that there `are indicia of reliability which have been widely viewed as determinative of whether a statement may be placed before the jury though there is no confrontation of the declarant, and to `afford the trier of fact a satisfactory basis for evaluating [*66] the truth of the prior statement'. It is clear from these statements, and from numerous prior decisions of this Court, that even though the witness be unavailable his prior testimony must bear some of these `indicia of reliability.'"

The Court has applied this "indicia of reliability" requirement principally by concluding that certain hearsay exceptions rest upon such solid foundations that admission of virtually any evidence within them comports with the "substance of the constitutional protection." This reflects the truism that "hearsay rules and the Confrontation Clause are generally designed to protect similar values," and "stem from the same roots." It also responds to the need for certainty in the workaday world of conducting criminal trials.

In sum, when a hearsay declarant is not present for cross-examination at trial, the Confrontation Clause normally requires a showing that he is unavailable. Even then, his statement is admissible only if it bears adequate "indicia of reliability." Reliability can be inferred without more in a case where the evidence falls within a firmly rooted hearsay exception. In other cases, the evidence must be excluded, at least absent a showing of particularized guarantees of trustworthiness.

III

We turn first to that aspect of confrontation analysis deemed dispositive by the Supreme Court of Ohio, and [*68] answered by it in the negative—whether Anita Isaacs' prior testimony at the preliminary hearing bore sufficient "indicia of reliability." Resolution of this issue requires a careful comparison of this case to California v. Green, supra.

A

In Green, at the preliminary hearing, a youth named Porter identified Green as a drug supplier. When called to the stand at Green's trial, however, Porter professed a lapse of memory. Frustrated in its attempt to adduce live testimony, the prosecution offered Porter's prior statements. The trial judge ruled the evidence admissible, and substantial portions of the preliminary hearing transcript were read to the jury. This Court found no error. Citing the established rule that prior trial testimony is admissible upon retrial if the declarant becomes unavailable, and recent dicta suggesting the admissibility of preliminary hearing testimony under proper circumstances, the Court rejected Green's Confrontation Clause attack. It reasoned:

"Porter's statement at the preliminary hearing had already been given under circumstances closely approximating those that surround the typical trial. Porter was under oath; respondent was represented by counsel—the same counsel in fact who later represented him at the trial; respondent had every opportunity to cross-examine Porter as to his statement; and the proceedings were conducted before a judicial tribunal, equipped to provide a judicial record of the hearings."

These factors, the Court concluded, provided all that the Sixth Amendment demands: "substantial compliance with the purposes behind the confrontation requirement."

This passage and others in the Green opinion suggest that the opportunity to cross- examine at the preliminary hearing— even absent actual cross-examination—satisfies the Confrontation Clause. Yet the record showed, and the Court recognized, that defense counsel in fact had cross-examined Porter at the earlier proceeding. Thus, MR. JUSTICE BRENNAN, writing in dissent, could conclude only that "perhaps" "the mere opportunity for face-to-face encounter is sufficient."

We need not decide whether the Supreme Court of Ohio correctly dismissed statements in Green suggesting that the mere opportunity to cross-examine rendered the prior testimony admissible. Nor need we decide whether de minimis questioning is sufficient, for defense counsel in this case tested Anita's testimony with the equivalent of significant cross-examination.

B

Counsel's questioning clearly partook of cross-examination as a matter of form. His presentation was replete with leading questions, the principal tool and hallmark of cross-examination. In addition, counsel's questioning comported with the principal purpose of cross- examination: to challenge "whether the declarant was sincerely telling what he believed to be the truth, whether the declarant accurately perceived and remembered the matter he related, and whether the declarant's intended meaning is adequately conveyed by the language he employed." Davenport, The Confrontation Clause and the Co-Conspirator Exception in Criminal Prosecutions: A Functional Analysis, 85 Harv. L. Rev. 1378 (1972).

Anita's unwillingness to shift the blame away from respondent became discernible early in her testimony. Yet counsel continued to explore the underlying events in detail. He attempted, for example, to establish that Anita and respondent were sharing an apartment, an assertion that was critical to respondent's defense at trial and that might have suggested ulterior personal reasons for unfairly casting blame on respondent. At another point, he directly challenged Anita's veracity by seeking to have her admit that she had given the credit cards to respondent to obtain a television. When Anita denied this, defense counsel elicited the fact that the only television she owned was a "Twenty Dollar . . . old model."

Respondent argues that, because defense counsel never asked the court to declare Anita hostile, his questioning necessarily occurred on direct examination. But however, state law might formally characterize the questioning of Anita, it afforded "substantial compliance with the purposes behind the confrontation requirement," no less so than classic cross-examination. Although Ohio law may have authorized objection by the prosecutor or intervention by the court, this did not happen. As in Green, respondent's counsel was not "significantly limited in any way in the scope or nature of his cross- examination."

We are also unpersuaded that Green is distinguishable on the ground that Anita Isaacs — unlike the declarant Porter in Green— was not personally available for questioning at trial. This argument ignores the language and logic of Green:

"Porter's statement would, we think, have been admissible at trial even in Porter's absence if Porter had been actually unavailable. . . . That being the case, we do not think a different result should follow where the witness is actually produced."

Nor does it matter that, unlike Green, respondent had a different lawyer at trial from the one at the preliminary hearing. Although one might strain one's reading of Green to assign this factor some significance, respondent advances no reason of substance supporting the distinction. Indeed, if we were to accept this suggestion, Green would carry the seeds of its own demise; under a "same attorney" rule, a defendant could nullify the effect of Green by obtaining new counsel after the preliminary hearing was concluded.

Finally, we reject respondent's attempt to fall back on general principles of confrontation, and his argument that this case falls among those in which the Court must undertake a particularized search for "indicia of reliability." Under this theory, the factors previously cited—absence of face-to-face contact at trial, presence of a new attorney, and the lack of classic cross-examination—combine with considerations uniquely tied to Anita to mandate exclusion of her statements. Anita, respondent says, had every reason to lie to avoid prosecution or parental reprobation. Her unknown whereabouts is explicable as an effort to avoid punishment, perjury, or self- incrimination. Given these facts, her prior testimony falls on the unreliable side, and should have been excluded.

In making this argument, respondent in effect asks us to disassociate preliminary hearing testimony previously subjected to cross-examination from previously cross- examined prior-trial testimony, which the Court has deemed generally immune from subsequent confrontation attack. Precedent requires us to decline this invitation. In Green the Court found guarantees of trustworthiness in the accouterments of the preliminary hearing itself; there was no mention of the inherent reliability or unreliability of Porter and his story.

In sum, we perceive no reason to resolve the reliability issue differently here than the Court did in Green. "Since there was an adequate opportunity to cross-examine [the witness], and counsel . . . availed himself of that opportunity, the transcript . . . bore sufficient `indicia of reliability' and afforded `"the trier of fact a satisfactory basis for evaluating the truth of the prior statement."

IV

Our holding that the Supreme Court of Ohio erred in its "indicia of reliability" analysis does not fully dispose of the case, for respondent would defend the judgment on an alternative ground. The State, he contends, failed to lay a proper predicate for admission of the preliminary hearing transcript by its failure to demonstrate that Anita Isaacs was not available to testify in person at the trial. All the justices of the Supreme Court of Ohio rejected this argument.

A

The basic litmus of Sixth Amendment unavailability is established: "[A] witness is not `unavailable' for purposes of . . . the exception to the confrontation requirement unless the prosecutorial authorities have made a good-faith effort to obtain his presence at trial."

Although it might be said that the Court's prior cases provide no further refinement of this statement of the rule, certain general propositions safely emerge. The law does not require the doing of a futile act. Thus, if no possibility of procuring the witness exists (as, for example, the witness' intervening death), "good faith" demands nothing of the prosecution. But if there is a possibility, albeit remote, that affirmative measures might produce the declarant, the obligation of good faith may demand their effectuation. "The lengths to which the prosecution must go to produce a witness. . . is a question of reasonableness." The ultimate question is whether the witness is unavailable despite good-faith efforts undertaken prior to trial to locate and present that witness. As with other evidentiary proponents, the prosecution bears the burden of establishing this predicate.

B

On the facts presented we hold that the trial court and the Supreme Court of Ohio correctly concluded that Anita's unavailability, in the constitutional sense, was established.

At the voir dire hearing, called for by the defense, it was shown that some four months prior to the trial the prosecutor was in touch with Amy Isaacs and discussed with her Anita's whereabouts.

It may appropriately be inferred that Mrs. Isaacs told the prosecutor essentially the same facts to which she testified at voir dire: that the Isaacs had last heard from Anita during the preceding summer; that she was not then in San Francisco, but was traveling outside Ohio; and that the Isaacs and their other children knew of no way to reach Anita even in an emergency. This last fact takes on added significance when it is recalled that Anita's parents earlier had undertaken affirmative efforts to reach their daughter when the social worker's inquiry came in from San Francisco. This is not a case of parents abandoning all interest in an absent daughter.

The evidence of record demonstrates that the prosecutor issued a subpoena to Anita at her parents' home, not only once, but on five separate occasions over a period of several months. In addition, at the voir dire argument, the prosecutor stated to the court that respondent "witnessed that I have attempted to locate, I have subpoenaed, there has been a voir dire of the witness' parents, and they have not been able to locate her for over a year."

Given these facts, the prosecution did not breach its duty of good-faith effort.

To be sure, the prosecutor might have tried to locate by telephone the San Francisco social worker with whom Mrs. Isaacs had spoken many months before and might have undertaken other steps in an effort to find Anita.

One, in hindsight, may always think of other things. Nevertheless, the great improbability that such efforts would have resulted in locating the witness, and would have led to her production at trial, neutralizes any intimation that a concept of reasonableness required their execution. We accept as a general rule, of course, the proposition that "the possibility of a refusal is not the equivalent of asking and receiving a rebuff." But the service and ineffectiveness of the five subpoenas and the conversation with Anita's mother were far more than mere reluctance to face the possibility of a refusal. It was investigation at the last-known real address, and it was conversation with a parent who was concerned about her daughter's whereabouts.

Barber and Mancusi v. Stubbs, supra, are the cases in which this Court has explored the issue of constitutional unavailability.

Although each is factually distinguishable from this case, Mancusi provides significant support for a conclusion of good-faith effort here, [13] and Barber has no contrary significance.

Insofar as this record discloses no basis for concluding that Anita was abroad, the case is factually weaker than Mancusi; but it is stronger than Mancusi in the sense that the Ohio prosecutor, unlike the prosecutor in Mancusi, had no clear indication, if any at all, of Anita's whereabouts.

In Barber, the Court found an absence of good-faith effort where the prosecution made no attempt to secure the presence of a declarant incarcerated in a federal penitentiary in a neighboring State.

There, the prosecution knew where the witness was, procedures existed whereby the witness could be brought to the trial, and the witness was not in a position to frustrate efforts to secure his production. Here, Anita's whereabouts were not known, and there was no assurance that she would be found in a place from which she could be forced to return to Ohio.

We conclude that the prosecution carried its burden of demonstrating that Anita was constitutionally unavailable for purposes of respondent's trial.

The judgment of the Supreme Court of Ohio is reversed, and the case is remanded for further proceedings not inconsistent with this opinion.

It is so ordered.

MR. JUSTICE BRENNAN, with whom MR. JUSTICE MARSHALL and MR. JUSTICE STEVENS join, dissenting.

The Court concludes that because Anita Isaacs' testimony at respondent's preliminary hearing was subjected to the equivalent of significant cross-examination, such hearsay evidence bore sufficient "indicia of reliability" to permit its introduction at respondent's trial without offending the Confrontation Clause of the Sixth Amendment. As the Court recognizes, however, the Constitution imposes the threshold requirement that the prosecution must demonstrate the unavailability of the witness whose prerecorded testimony it wishes to use against the defendant. Because I cannot agree that the State has met its burden of establishing this predicate, I dissent. "There are few subjects, perhaps, upon which this Court and other courts have been more nearly unanimous than in their expressions of belief that the right of confrontation and cross-examination is an essential and fundamental requirement for the kind of fair trial which is this country's constitutional goal.

"Historically, the inclusion of the Confrontation Clause in the Bill of Rights reflected the Framers' conviction that the defendant must not be denied the opportunity to challenge his accusers in a direct encounter before the trier of fact.

At the heart of this constitutional guarantee is the accused's right to compel the witness "to stand face to face with the jury in order that they may look at him, and judge by his demeanor upon the stand and the manner in which he gives his testimony whether he is worthy of belief."

Despite the literal language of the Sixth Amendment, our cases have recognized the necessity for a limited exception to the confrontation requirement for the prior testimony of a witness who is unavailable at the defendant's trial.

In keeping with the importance of this provision in our constitutional scheme, however, we have imposed a heavy burden on the prosecution either to secure the presence of the witness or to demonstrate the impossibility of that endeavor. Barber v. Page, supra, held that the absence of a witness from the jurisdiction does not excuse the State's failure to attempt to compel the witness' attendance at trial; in such circumstances, the government must show that it has engaged in a diligent effort to locate and procure the witness' return. "In short, a witness is not `unavailable' for purposes of the foregoing exception to the confrontation requirement unless the prosecutorial authorities have made a good-faith effort to obtain his presence at trial."

In the present case, I am simply unable to conclude that the prosecution met its burden of establishing Anita Isaacs' unavailability. From all that appears in the record—and there has been no suggestion that the record is incomplete in this respect—the State's total effort to secure Anita's attendance at respondent's trial consisted of the delivery of five subpoenas in her name to her parents' residence, and three of those were issued after the authorities had learned that she was no longer living there.

At least four months before the trial began, the prosecution was aware that Anita had moved away; yet during that entire interval it did nothing whatsoever to try to make contact with her. It is difficult to believe that the State would have been so derelict in attempting to secure the witness' presence at trial had it not had her favorable preliminary hearing testimony upon which to rely in the event of her "unavailability." The perfunctory steps which the State took in this case can hardly qualify as a "good-faith effort." In point of fact, it was no effort at all.

The Court, however, is apparently willing to excuse the prosecution's inaction on the ground that any endeavor to locate Anita Isaacs was unlikely to bear fruit. I not only take issue with the premise underlying that reasoning—that the improbability of success can condone a refusal to conduct even a cursory investigation into the witness' whereabouts— but I also seriously question the Court's conclusion that a bona fide search in the present case would inevitably have come to naught.

Surely the prosecution's mere speculation about the difficulty of locating Anita Isaacs cannot relieve it of the obligation to attempt to find her. Although the rigor of the undertaking might serve to palliate a failure to prevail, it cannot justify a failure even to try.

Just as Barber cautioned that "the possibility of a refusal is not the equivalent of asking and receiving a rebuff," so, too, the possibility of a defeat is not the equivalent of pursuing all obvious leads and returning empty-handed. The duty of "good-faith effort" would be meaningless indeed "if that effort were required only in circumstances where success was guaranteed."

Nor do I concur in the Court's bleak prognosis of the likelihood of procuring Anita Isaacs' attendance at respondent's trial. Although Anita's mother testified that she had no current knowledge of her daughter's whereabouts, the prosecution possessed sufficient information upon which it could have at least initiated an investigation.

As the Court acknowledges, one especially promising lead was the San Francisco social worker to whom Mrs. Isaacs had spoken and with whom Anita had filed for welfare.

What the Court fails to mention, however, is that the prosecution had more to go on than that datum alone. For example, Mrs. Isaacs testified that on the same day she talked to the social worker, she also spoke to her daughter.

And although Mrs. Isaacs told defense counsel that she knew of no way to get in touch with her daughter in an emergency, in response to a similar question from the prosecutor she indicated that someone in Tucson might be able to contact Anita.

It would serve no purpose here to essay an exhaustive catalog of the numerous measures the State could have taken in a diligent attempt to locate Anita. It suffices simply to note that it is not "hindsight," that permits us to envision how a skilled investigator armed with this information (and any additional facts not brought out through the voir dire) might have discovered Anita's whereabouts with reasonable effort. Indeed, precisely because the prosecution did absolutely nothing to try to locate Anita, hindsight does not enhance the vista of investigatory opportunities that were available to the State had it actually attempted to find her.

In sum, what the Court said in Barber v. Page, 390 U. S., at 725, is equally germane here: "[S]o far as this record reveals, the sole reason why [the witness] was not present to testify in person was because the State did not attempt to seek [her] presence. The right of confrontation may not be dispensed with so lightly."

CASE 3 - SPOUSAL PRIVILEGE

IN THE UNITED STATES DISTRICT COURT FOR THE DISTRICT OF HAWAII
UNITED STATES OF AMERICA, Plaintiff,

vs.

PERRY ARTATES, Defendant.

CR. NO. 12-00826-02 SOM ORDER AFFIRMING MAGISTRATE) JUDGE'S REFUSAL TO SEVER

ORDER AFFIRMING MAGISTRATE JUDGE'S REFUSAL TO SEVER TRIAL

I. INTRODUCTION.

Defendant Perry Artates and his wife are jointly charged with conspiracy, wire fraud, and falsifying information on a loan application. Artates moved to sever his trial from that of his wife under Rule 14(a) of the Federal Rules of Criminal Procedure. Stating that he wished to testify in his own defense without implicating his wife in the process, Artates sought to sever their trials, apparently concluding that he would not then be forced to choose between testifying in his own defense and asserting his spousal privilege. Magistrate Judge Barry M. Kurren denied Artates's motion for severance ("Order"). Artates appeals. This court AFFIRMS the thoughtful and well-reasoned Order.

II. STANDARD FOR APPEAL OF PRETRIAL MATTER DETERMINED BY MAGISTRATE JUDGE.

Pursuant to 28 U.S.C. § 636(b)(1) and Criminal Local Rule 57.3(b), a party may appeal to a district judge any pretrial non-dispositive matter determined by a magistrate judge. Under 28 U.S.C. § 636(b)(1)(A), a magistrate judge's order may be reversed by the district court only if it is "clearly erroneous or contrary to law."

III. ANALYSIS.

Rule 8(b) of the Federal Rules of Criminal Procedure governs the proper joinder of defendants. Under Rule 8(b), "[t]he indictment or information may charge two or more defendants if they are alleged to have participated in the same act or transaction, or in the same series of acts or transactions, constituting an offense or offenses."

A co-defendant may seek severance of a joint trial under Rule 14(a), which provides, "[i]f the joinder of . . . defendants in an indictment . . . appears to prejudice a defendant . . . the court may . . . sever the defendants' trials . . . ."

The Supreme Court has recognized a preference for joint trials in the federal system when defendants are indicted together. Zafiro v. United States, 506 U.S. 534, 537 (1993).

Joint trials promote efficiency and "generally serve the interests of justice by avoiding inconsistent verdicts and enabling more accurate assessment of relative culpability."

In Zafiro, the petitioners urged the Court to adopt a bright-line rule mandating severance whenever codefendants have conflicting defenses.

The Supreme Court declined to do so, explaining that mutually antagonistic defenses are not per se prejudicial, and that the district court has the discretion to determine the relief to be granted. The Court stated,

When defendants properly have been joined under Rule 8(b), a district court should grant severance under Rule 14 only if there is a serious risk that a joint trial would compromise a specific trial right of one of the defendants or prevent the jury from making a reliable judgment about guilt or innocence.

A. The Spousal Privilege Does Not Mandate Severance of Artates's Trial.

Artates argues that his privilege against giving adverse spousal testimony is a specific trial right that would be compromised in a joint trial. Magistrate Judge Kurren correctly reasoned that the privilege against adverse spousal testimony is not a specific trial right that warrants severance under Rule 14.

Artates also argues on appeal that the privilege essentially interferes with his fundamental right to testify at trial. He states that being forced to choose between his spousal privilege and testifying in his own defense has a chilling effect on his constitutional right to testify. This court adopts the Magistrate Judge's reasoning concerning why Artates's fundamental right to testify remains intact.

Artates's retention of the right to testify in his own defense is highlighted by the request in his original motion that

"his trial be subsequent to the trial of his co-defendant spouse." Artates is implicitly saying that he has no problem exercising his right to testify and waiving the spousal privilege provided his testimony does not prejudice his spouse, who will have already been tried. What is at issue is not really a tension between his right to testify and his spousal privilege, but the tension between the success of his defense and the success of his spouse's defense. Unfortunately for Artates, severance is not a remedy designed to address that tension.

In the first place, severance itself does not go to the order in which Defendants are tried. If severance were ordered and Artates were tried first, he could still testify. However, if his testimony included evidence incriminating his wife, he would have waived any privilege as to that evidence and could not hide behind the privilege in the subsequent trial of his wife.

Even if severance were ordered and Artates's wife were tried first, it is not at all clear that severance would address Artates's dilemma. If the wife were convicted and contemplated an appeal, Artates's testimony in his own defense in his own trial could constitute a waiver of the spousal privilege that might require him to testify against his wife if the Ninth circuit remanded her case for retrial. In short, severance is not a remedy for the situation Artates is in.

B. Artates Does Not Demonstrate That He Would Suffer Undue Prejudice in a Joint Trial.

The Supreme Court considered a defendant's risk of prejudice, for purposes of Rule 14, as involving a factual determination to be evaluated on a case-by-case basis. This court has examined Artates's public and sealed declarations concerning his possible trial testimony. As this court noted earlier in the present order, the evidence concerns possible prejudice to his wife, not himself. Artates fails to demonstrate that he himself would suffer undue prejudice in a joint trial.

The Supreme Court in Zafiro recognized that "a defendant might suffer prejudice if essential exculpatory evidence that would be available to a defendant tried alone were unavailable in a joint trial." Artates's possible testimony exonerating himself is by no means unavailable in a joint trial. Artates himself has the power to present it. A decision to waive the spousal privilege is akin to the decision by any alleged co-conspirator to offer exculpatory testimony in his own defense, while incriminating his co-defendant, who might be his own child or parent or sibling.

This court sees nothing in the Magistrate Judge's Order that is clearly erroneous or contrary to law.

IV. CONCLUSION.

The court AFFIRMS Magistrate Judge Kurren's Order denying Artates's motion to sever his trial from his wife's.

IT IS SO ORDERED.
DATED: Honolulu, Hawaii, January 25, 2013.
Susan Oki Mollway - Chief United States District Judge

CASE 4 - EVIDENCE OF OTHER CRIMES

UNITED STATES COURT OF APPEALS FOR THE THIRD CIRCUIT   No. 07-3819

UNITED STATES OF AMERICA, v.
STEVEN LANE,
Appellant.

Appeal from the United States District Court for the Eastern District of Pennsylvania No. 04-cr-00697-2

(District Judge: The Honorable William H. Yohn)
Submitted Pursuant to Third Circuit LAR 34.1(a) June 2, 2009

Before: McKEE, HARDIMAN, and GREENBERG Circuit Judges (Filed August 14, 2009)

NOT PRECEDENTIAL
Case: 07-3819 Document: 00319769644 Page: 2 Date Filed: 08/14/2009
OPINION OF THE COURT

McKee, Circuit Judge,
Steven Lane appeals his conviction for conspiracy to interfere with interstate commerce by robbery under 18 U.S.C. § 1951(a). For the reasons that follow, we will affirm.

I.

Inasmuch as we are writing primarily for the parties who are familiar with this case, we need not recite the factual or procedural history.

Lane argues that the district court erred in permitting a government witness to testify about Lane's involvement in a prior robbery for which he had been neither charged nor convicted. He contends that this testimony was irrelevant and that its probative value was outweighed by its prejudicial effect, and that he is therefore entitled to a new trial under Fed. R. Evid. 404(b). We disagree.

We review the district court's decision to admit evidence for abuse of discretion. Rule 404(b) states that while "[e]vidence of other crimes, wrongs, or acts is not admissible to prove the character of a person in order to show conformity therewith," such evidence may be used for other purposes. Indeed, such evidence shall be admitted "if relevant for any other purpose than to show a mere propensity or disposition on the part of the defendant to commit the crime."

In order to be admissible under Rule 404(b), evidence must meet four requirements: (1) it must be offered for a proper purpose; (2) it must be relevant; (3) its probative value must not be substantially outweighed by any unfair prejudicial impact; and (4) the court must properly instruct the jury about the proper use and relevance of the evidence.

During argument on the motion to introduce this evidence the government explained that the testimony about the prior robbery was necessary to establish the ongoing relationship of Lane with his co-defendant, the government's witness.

The testimony explained why Lane and the co- defendant trusted each other and were able to accomplish the robbery in question without significant planning. The evidence was therefore relevant to establishing preparation and plan which are appropriate uses of evidence of a defendant's prior "bad acts" under Rule 404(b). Moreover, this testimony was the only way the government could establish the relationship between Lane and the co-defendant, and that was certainly relevant to the government's case. Accordingly, the district court correctly found that a "genuine need" for the evidence outweighed any prejudicial effect.

We have held in numerous cases that evidence of prior criminal activity is admissible under Rule 404(b) to show the relationship between a witness and a defendant. See, e.g., United States v. Butch, (allowing witness in pharmaceutical theft case to testify as to defendant's prior participation in identical theft); see also United States v. Simmons, 679 F.2d 1042, 1050 (3d Cir. 1982), cert. denied, 462 U.S. 1134 (1983) (holding that evidence may be introduced "to provide necessary background information, to show an ongoing relationship between [the defendant and a co-conspirator], and to help the jury understand the co- conspirator's role in the scheme").

In addition, the district court gave an appropriate limiting instruction to the jury that minimized the likelihood that the evidence would be considered for an improper purpose.

Given the district court's limiting instruction, and the relevance of the evidence under Rule 404(b), we find no error at all in admitting this evidence, let alone any "plain error."

The instruction was given both at the time of the testimony, and again before the jury deliberated. There is nothing in the record to suggest that the jury did not understand the instructions or were incapable of following them.

Although Lane cites several cases to support his argument that the instructions were insufficient to overcome the prejudicial effect of the testimony, all of the cases he cites involve situations where there was either no proper purpose for the evidence, or the court simply failed to give any limiting instruction at all. Here, "we believe this is a case where the jury could be expected to compartmentalize the evidence and consider it for its proper purposes."

II.

For all of the above reasons, we will affirm the judgment of conviction.

CASE 5 - EXPERT WITNESS

UNITED STATES DISTRICT COURT EASTERN DISTRICT OF TENNESSEE AT KNOXVILLE

UNITED STATES OF AMERICA, Plaintiff, v.
MARK A. TINDELL, Defendant. MEMORANDUM AND ORDER

All pretrial motions in this case have been referred to the undersigned pursuant to 28 636(b) for disposition or report and recommendation regarding disposition by the district U.S.C. §court as may be appropriate.

This matter before the Court upon the Defendant Mark A. Tindell's ("Tindell") Motion to Exclude Testimony and Evidence specifically, expert testimony proposed by the government. The government has provided notice that it intends to present the testimony of Special

Agent Dave Lewis of the D.E.A. the trial of this matter. Tindell objects to the testimony of Lewis, citing Daubert v. Merrell Dow Pharmaceuticals, Inc., 509 U.S. 579 (1993).

According to Tindell, the government proposes to offer Lewis as an expert witness at trial and has described what Lewis' testimony is expected to show [Doc. 105]. Tindell objects to Lewis as an expert generally, and in particular to his testimony to two conclusions: that the circumstances surrounding Tindell's possession of oxycodone is consistent with distribution and inconsistent with personal use; and that the firearm found on Tindell is consistent with a firearm used during, and in relation to, a drug crime.

In 1993 the United States Supreme Court changed the standard for admission of expert testimony in federal courts with its decision in Daubert v. Merrell Dow Pharmaceuticals, Inc., 509 U.S. 579 (1993). The Court in Daubert held that Rule 702 of the Federal Rules of Evidence requires a trial court to ensure that scientific testimony is relevant and reliable. Daubert, 509 U.S. at 589.

Rule 702 of the Federal Rules of Evidence provides as follows:

If scientific, technical, or other specialized knowledge will assist the trier of fact to understand the evidence or to determine a fact in issue, a witness qualified as an expert by knowledge, skill, experience, training, or education, may testify thereto in the form of an opinion or otherwise, if (1) the testimony is based upon sufficient facts or data, (2) the testimony is the product of reliable principles and methods, and (3) the witness has applied the principles and methods reliably to the facts of the case.

The Daubert opinion enumerated non-exclusive factors to guide the trial court's consideration. The Daubert Court stated that its discussion was "limited to the scientific context," as opposed to "technical, or other specialized knowledge" to which Rule 702 also applies. The Sixth Circuit has consistently held that expert testimony by a law enforcement officer about the method of operation of drug dealers and the role of firearms in drug trafficking is admissible to "assist the trier of fact to understand the evidence or to determine a fact in issue." In fact, the Court observes that the Sixth Circuit has specifically addressed Special Agent David Lewis' qualifications as an expert in this context:

Here, the district court did not abuse its discretion because Agent Lewis, a qualified law enforcement agent with 22 years of experience and extensive drug-investigation training, testified about illegal drug operations information beyond the ken of the average layman, and the district court gave the usual cautionary instruction regarding expert testimony.

In List, Agent Lewis testified "about how much drugs are worth on the street, how drug dealers sometimes use code words to disguise their transactions, how possession of large drug quantities indicates commercial rather than personal use, how drugs are packaged and shipped, and how drug dealers typically use and carry firearms."

The Sixth Circuit stated, "this court has held that drug-enforcement agents may testify as experts on the operations and characteristics of drug-trafficking organizations."

The Court finds that a Daubert hearing would not assist the trial court in determining the admissibility of this proposed expert's testimony. Accordingly, defendant Tindell's Motion is DENIED. This ruling does not limit defendant's ability to object to the testimony at trial should the government fail to lay a proper foundation or if any specific testimony is not relevant.

IT IS SO ORDERED.

ENTER:

H. Bruce Guyton United States Magistrate Judge

CASE 6 - CHARACTER

UNITED STATES OF AMERICA

v.

ARTHUR MICHAEL KINSELLA, Defendant.

CR-05-27-B-W

UNITED STATES DISTRICT COURT DISTRICT OF MAINE

ORDER ON CROSS-EXAMINATION OF CHARACTER WITNESSES

The Court grants the Defendant's motion in limine in part and rules that, if a proper foundation is established, character evidence may be admissible. The Court further describes the process by which character evidence may be admitted and cross- examined under Rule 405(a) and requires the prosecutor to approach the Court before cross-examining on specific instances of bad conduct.

I. STATEMENT OF FACTS

Arthur Michael Kinsella is proceeding to trial on the charge that, after being allowed to return to Canada on the condition that he appear as necessary at future court proceedings, he willfully failed to appear at his arraignment, an alleged violation of 18 U.S.C. § 3146(c).

In its trial brief, the Government raises the question as to the scope of permissible cross-examination of the Defendant's character witnesses. Government's Trial Br. at 6-7 (Docket # 120). The Government stated that it "anticipates that the defendant will seek to introduce character evidence and request a jury instruction regarding his alleged reputation for honesty, lawfulness or integrity in the community."

The Government objects to the admissibility of such character evidence, but if allowed, it seeks a ruling that would allow it on cross-examination to rebut this evidence with "evidence of bad character pursuant to Rule 404(a)(1) of the Federal Rules of Evidence." Mr. Kinsella is currently under indictment on two drug charges and the Government seeks to cross-examine the character witnesses on their knowledge of "the defendant's history in Canada and his distribution and possession with intent to distribute oxycodone and Oxycontin."

After the Government filed its trial brief, Mr. Kinsella moved in limine to "supervise closely the prosecutor's cross-examination of reputation witnesses (as opposed to opinion witnesses) regarding specific acts of misconduct." Mr. Kinsella reveals that he intends to present evidence that he holds a good reputation for lawfulness in his community and he cites First Circuit law as holding such evidence generally admissible in a criminal case. However, Mr. Kinsella contends that to allow the Government to question character witnesses about specific bad acts would create an "obvious prejudice." He says that before the Government may cross-examine on specific bad acts, it must "demonstrate a good faith factual basis for the incidents . . . [and] the incidents must be relevant to the character traits at issue in the case." He argues that the "specific instances of illegal conduct to which the Government refers in its trial brief appear to be suspicions held by the local constabulary regarding associations Mr. Kinsella may have had with others who are violating certain laws, but the exact nature of the information is uncertain."

II. DISCUSSION

Rule 404 creates an exception to the general exclusion of character evidence, when the evidence is "of a pertinent trait or character offered by an accused."(describing the modern rules governing the admissibility of character evidence as "counterintuitive and enigmatic vestiges of an ancient time"). The First Circuit has stated that evidence of a defendant's character as a law-abiding person is admissible "[w]ith very few exceptions." Angelini explained that "[e]vidence that [a defendant] was a law-abiding person would tend to make it less likely that he would knowingly break the law." Id. at 381. This inference is equally applicable in this case, where the Government is alleging that Mr. Kinsella willfully failed to appear at his arraignment. The Court overrules the Government's objection to the admissibility of reputation evidence.

A defendant introduces reputation evidence at a price. In cases where evidence of a person's character is admissible, Rule 405 provides that "[p]roof may be made by testimony as to reputation or by testimony in the form of an opinion." But, Rule 405 also allows inquiry on cross-examination "into relevant specific instances of conduct." Id. Whether cross-examination on "specific instances of conduct" is allowable under Rule 405(a) differs from whether prior bad acts would be admissible under Rule 404(b).

The seminal case on Rule 405 is Michelson v. United States, 335 U.S. 469 (1948). In Michelson, the Supreme Court noted that under common law, the Government may not produce "any kind of evidence of a defendant's evil character to establish a probability of his guilt." However, the line of inquiry "firmly denied to the State is opened to the defendant because character is relevant in resolving probabilities of guilt.

He may introduce affirmative testimony that the general estimate of his character is so favorable that the jury may infer that he would not be likely to commit the offense charged." But, the "price a defendant must pay for attempting to prove his good name is to throw open the entire subject which the law has kept closed for his benefit and to make himself vulnerable where the law otherwise shields him."

The defendant's witness is "subject to cross-examination as to the contents and extent of the hearsay on which he bases his conclusions . . . ." This process "subjects his proof to tests of credibility designed to prevent him from profiting by a mere parade of partisans."

A defendant is thus permitted to call a witness, establish his contemporaneous and relevant knowledge of the defendant's reputation, and elicit a favorable response. He is not permitted to ask questions about specific instances of good conduct or about specific character traits. ("The witness may not testify about defendant's specific acts or courses of conduct or his possession of a particular disposition or of benign mental and moral traits . . . .").

On cross-examination, the Government may inquire about specific instances of bad conduct; in Franklin's case, for example, his alleged possession of a truckload of stolen light bulbs. ("On cross-examination, however, the prosecution may ask defendant's character witnesses whether they have heard about or know about specific acts committed by defendant in order to test their knowledge and standards for good reputation.").

Franklin describes direct-examination:
Q. All right, sir. Do you know-well, tell me how long you have known Mr. Franklin, here, please sir?
A. Approximately two and a half years.
Q. Do you know his reputation in the community in which he lives and which he does business? A. I know of his business with our community and it has been excellent. We have extended considerable amount of credit which has been satisfactory.
Q. All right, sir. As far as his reputation and what you know of it, what would be your answer? A. Excellent.

Franklin describes cross-examination:

Q. Your reputation-your comments about his reputation-sir, were strictly with your business dealings with him, is that correct?
A. Yes, sir.
Q. Have you heard, sir, that Mr. Franklin back here had a truckload of light bulbs in his possession?

The commentators to Rule 405 describe the process. See Fed. R. Evid. 405, commentary by S.A. Saltzburg, D.J. Capra, & M.M. Martin (Lexis 2008). A prosecutor asks, for example, "Have you heard that the defendant committed a murder three years ago?"

If the witness has not heard of it, then an implication is created that he is not sufficiently qualified to attest to the defendant's reputation in the community. If the witness has heard about the specific act, and still testifies to the defendant's good reputation in the community, then an implication is created that the community itself is suspect, or that the witness is lying about the good reputation.

Id. The specific acts must be relevant to the offense and the Government must have a good faith basis for the incidents. Monteleone, the admission of Rule 405(a) evidence is often accompanied by a limiting instruction.

Here, the Defendant is unaware precisely what specific instances the Government intends to use on cross-examination. With this explanation for the process in mind, the better practice is for Government's counsel to approach the Court before engaging in cross-examination and to describe his good faith basis for asking the question and the relevance to the underlying case.

III. CONCLUSION

The Court grants the Defendant's motion in limine in part. If the Defendant establishes a proper foundation for character evidence, the Court will allow witnesses to testify under Rule 405(a). Before the Government cross-examines on any specific instance of bad conduct, it must approach the Court and explain its good faith basis for the question and its relevance to the underlying case.

SO ORDERED.
Dated this 8th day of April, 2008

/s/ John A. Woodcock, Jr.
JOHN A. WOODCOCK, JR.   UNITED STATES DISTRICT JUDGE

CASE 7 - BUSINESS RECORDS

UNITED STATES DISTRICT COURT FOR THE DISTRICT OF COLUMBIA
Criminal Nos. 11-129-1, 2, 11 (CKK)
MEMORANDUM OPINION

(November 15, 2012)

Before trial commenced, the Government filed a Notice of Intent to Introduce Certified Business Records in Evidence, indicating that the Government intended to introduce certified business records into evidence by way of authenticating declarations pursuant to Federal Rules of Evidence 803(6) and 902(11).

Among other objections from the Defendants, Defendant Williams objected on the grounds that the Rule 902(11) certifications purporting to authenticate the business records were testimonial and thus inadmissible hearsay pursuant to Crawford v. Washington, 541 U.S. 36 (2004). The Court overruled the Defendants' Crawford objection and resolved the parties' substantive objections to the records and certifications. The Government subsequently introduced certain records at trial with the certifications. This Memorandum Opinion briefly sets forth the Court's reasons for overruling the Defendants' Crawford objection.

I. BACKGROUND

Federal Rule of Evidence 803(6) provides that records made under certain conditions, often referred to as "business records," are not excluded by the prohibition on hearsay testimony.

UNITED STATES OF AMERICA, v.
GEZO GOEONG EDWARDS, et al., Defendants.

Under Rule 902(11), business records described in Rule 803(6) are self-authenticating if accompanied by a certification indicating the records meet the requirements of Rule 803(6). Pursuant to these rules, the Government filed a notice indicating it would seek to introduce a variety of business records (including bank records, rental car records, and cellular phone records) by way of authenticating certifications - declarations under oath from the relevant custodian of records.

Prior to 2004, there would have been little dispute that the Government could use this procedure so long as it satisfied the requirements of Rule 803(6) and 902(11). However, in Crawford v. Washington, 541 U.S. 36 (2004), the Supreme Court held that testimonial statements of witnesses that do not appear at trial violate the Confrontation Clause of the Sixth Amendment unless the witness is unavailable to testify, and the defendant had a previous opportunity to cross-examine the witness. The challenge for the courts since Crawford is to determine whether out of court statements otherwise admissible under the Federal Rules of Evidence---including the certifications are issue here---are testimonial and now inadmissible.

II. DISCUSSION

The thrust of Defendant Williams' argument is that the certifications are out of court statements made with the intent that the certifications would be used at trial in order to establish certain facts at trial. Thus, according to the Defendant, these certifications fall squarely within the scope of "testimonial" statements proscribed by Crawford. Although the D.C. Circuit has yet to directly rule on this issue, at least five other Circuits have rejected the Defendant's argument and concluded that certifications authenticating business records are not testimonial and therefore are not barred by Crawford. E.g., United States v. Johnson, 688 F.3d 494, 504-05 (8th Cir. 2012); United States v. Yeley- Davis, 632 F.3d 673, 680-81 (10th Cir. 2011); United States v. Morgan, 505 F.3d 332, 339 (5th Cir. 2007); United States v. Weiland, 420 F.3d 1062, 1077 (9th Cir. 2005).

Admittedly, the certifications are out of court statements, and they are likely made in anticipation of litigation. The Defendant argues, relying solely on an unpublished decision from the District of Kansas, that the certifications are introduced for the purpose of establishing a particular fact, "namely that the proper foundation for the admission of the business record[s] exist[]." As the Seventh Circuit explained in United States v. Ellis, 460 F.3d 920 (7th Cir. 2006), an authenticating certification under Rule 902(11) is "nothing more than the custodian of records . . . attesting that the submitted documents are actually records kept in the ordinary course of business" and "merely establish the existence of the procedures necessary to create a business record." It is the underlying business records, not the certification, that are introduced to establish facts at trial.

As part of its Confrontation Clause jurisprudence, the Supreme Court has specifically distinguished affidavits or certificates authenticating records from other types of affidavits. the Court held that an affidavit stating that materials seized in connection with a criminal investigation were cocaine was testimonial. However, in responding to the dissent's concern that the holding would eviscerate the usefulness of Rule 902(11), the Court explained that "[a] clerk could by affidavit authenticate or provide a copy of an otherwise admissible record, but could not do what the analysts did here: create a record for the sole purpose of providing evidence against a defendant." The Defendant emphasizes a different portion of the Court's analysis, which indicated that "a clerk's certificate attesting to the fact that the clerk had searched for a particular record and failed to find it," would be substantive evidence against the evidence. The Government did not seek to or actually introduce any certificate to this effect; each of the certifications used by the Government in this case merely authenticated business records introduced into evidence.

In a footnote, the Defendant notes that this discussion in Melendez-Diaz referenced a clerk authenticating public records, rather than a custodian authenticating business records. This is a distinction without a difference. Both types of certifications involve an individual attesting to the authenticity of certain records. It is the records, not the certification, that are introduced as substantive evidence against the defendant during trial. The certifications at issue are simply "too far removed from the 'principal evil at which the Confrontation Clause was directed' to be considered testimonial."

III. CONCLUSION

Cognizant of the care with which the Supreme Court has approached the Confrontation Clause and the application of Crawford, this is not a close case. At least five separate Circuits have held that certifications used pursuant to Federal Rule of Evidence 902(11) to authenticate business records are not testimonial and can be used to lay a foundation for the admissibility of business records under Rule 803(6). The certifications merely establish the procedures through which the underlying records were made. The business records---not the certifications---are used to establish facts against the defendant at trial.

COLLEEN KOLLAR-KOTELLY UNITED STATES DISTRICT JUDGE

CASE 8 - HEARSAY

(Slip Opinion) OCTOBER TERM, 2014 1

Syllabus

NOTE: Where it is feasible, a syllabus (headnote) will be released, as is being done in connection with this case, at the time the opinion is issued. The syllabus constitutes no part of the opinion of the Court but has been prepared by the Reporter of Decisions for the convenience of the reader.

SUPREME COURT OF THE UNITED STATES

Syllabus

OHIO v. CLARK

CERTIORARI TO THE SUPREME COURT OF OHIO

No. 13–1352. Argued March 2, 2015—Decided June 18, 2015

Respondent Darius Clark sent his girlfriend away to engage in prostitution while he cared for her 3-year-old son L. P. and 18-month-old daughter A. T. When L. P.'s preschool teachers noticed marks on his body, he identified Clark as his abuser. Clark was subsequently tried on multiple counts related to the abuse of both children. At trial, the State introduced L. P.'s statements to his teachers as evidence of Clark's guilt, but L. P. did not testify. The trial court denied Clark's motion to exclude the statements under the Sixth Amendment's Confrontation Clause. A jury convicted Clark on all but one count. The state appellate court reversed the conviction on Confrontation Clause grounds, and the Supreme Court of Ohio affirmed.

Held: The introduction of L. P.'s statements at trial did not violate the Confrontation Clause.

(a) This Court's decision in Crawford v. Washington, 541 U. S. 36, 54, held that the Confrontation Clause generally prohibits the introduction of "testimonial" statements by a non-testifying witness, unless the witness is "unavailable to testify, and the defendant had had a prior opportunity for cross-examination." A statement qualifies as testimonial if the "primary purpose" of the conversation was to "create an out-of-court substitute for trial testimony." In making that "primary purpose" determination, courts must consider "all of the relevant circumstances." "Where no such primary purpose exists, the admissibility of a statement is the concern of state and federal rules of evidence, not the Confrontation Clause." But that does not mean that the Confrontation Clause bars every statement that satisfies the "primary purpose" test. The Court has recognized that the Confrontation Clause does not prohibit the introduction of out-of-court statements that would have been admissible in a criminal case at the time of the founding. Thus, the primary purpose test is a necessary, but not always sufficient, condition for the exclusion of out-of-court statements under the Confrontation Clause.

(b) Considering all the relevant circumstances, L. P.'s statements were not testimonial. L. P.'s statements were not made with the primary purpose of creating evidence for Clark's prosecution. They occurred in the context of an ongoing emergency involving suspected child abuse. L. P.'s teachers asked questions aimed at identifying and ending a threat. They did not inform the child that his answers would be used to arrest or punish his abuser. L. P. never hinted that he intended his statements to be used by the police or prosecutors. And the conversation was informal and spontaneous. L. P.'s age further confirms that the statements in question were not testimonial because statements by very young children will rarely, if ever, implicate the Confrontation Clause. As a historical matter, moreover, there is strong evidence that statements made in circumstances like these were regularly admitted at common law. Finally, although statements to individuals other than law enforcement officers are not categorically outside the Sixth Amendment's reach, the fact that L. P. was speaking to his teachers is highly relevant. Statements to individuals who are not principally charged with uncovering and prosecuting criminal behavior are significantly less likely to be testimonial than those given to law enforcement officers. (c) Clark's arguments to the contrary are unpersuasive. Mandatory reporting obligations do not convert a conversation between a concerned teacher and her student into a law enforcement mission aimed at gathering evidence for prosecution. It is irrelevant that the teachers' questions and their duty to report the matter had the natural tendency to result in Clark's prosecution. And this Court's Confrontation Clause decisions do not determine whether a statement is testimonial by examining whether a jury would view the statement as the equivalent of in-court testimony. Instead, the test is whether a statement was given with the "primary purpose of creating an out-ofcourt substitute for trial testimony." Here, the answer is clear: L. P.'s statements to his teachers were not testimonial.

137 Ohio St. 3d 346, 2013–Ohio–4731, 999 N. E. 2d 592, reversed and remanded.

ALITO, J., delivered the opinion of the Court, in which ROBERTS, C. J., and KENNEDY, BREYER, SOTOMAYOR, and KAGAN, joined. SCALIA,J., filed an opinion concurring in the judgment, in which GINSBURG, J., joined. THOMAS, J., filed an opinion concurring in the judgment.

Opinion of the Court
SUPREME COURT OF THE UNITED STATES
No. 13–1352
OHIO, PETITIONER v. DARIUS CLARK
ON WRIT OF CERTIORARI TO THE SUPREME COURT OF OHIO June 18, 2015
JUSTICE ALITO delivered the opinion of the Court.

Darius Clark sent his girlfriend hundreds of miles away to engage in prostitution and agreed to care for her two young children while she was out of town. A day later, teachers discovered red marks on her 3-year-old son, and the boy identified Clark as his abuser. The question in this case is whether the Sixth Amendment's Confrontation Clause prohibited prosecutors from introducing those statements when the child was not available to be cross-examined. Because neither the child nor his teachers had the primary purpose of assisting in Clark's prosecution, the child's statements do not implicate the Confrontation Clause and therefore were admissible at trial.

I

Darius Clark, who went by the nickname "Dee," lived in Cleveland, Ohio, with his girlfriend, T. T., and her two children: L. P., a 3-year-old boy, and A. T., an 18-month old girl.1 Clark was also T. T.'s pimp, and he would regularly send her on trips to Washington, D. C., to work as a prostitute. In March 2010, T. T. went on one such trip, and she left the children in Clark's care.

The next day, Clark took L. P. to preschool. In the lunchroom, one of L. P.'s teachers, Ramona Whitley, observed that L. P.'s left eye appeared bloodshot. She asked him "'what happened,'" and he initially said nothing. Eventually, however, he told the teacher that he "'fell.'" When they moved into the brighter lights of a classroom, Whitley noticed "'red marks, like whips of some sort,'" on L. P.'s face. Ibid. She notified the lead teacher, Debra Jones, who asked L. P., "'Who did this? What happened to you?'" I According to Jones, L. P. "'seemed kind of bewildered'" and " 'said something like, Dee, Dee.' " Jones asked L. P. whether Dee is "big or little," to which L. P. responded that "Dee is big." Jones then brought L. P. to her supervisor, who lifted the boy's shirt, revealing more injuries. Whitley called a child abuse hotline to alert authorities about the suspected abuse.

When Clark later arrived at the school, he denied responsibility for the injuries and quickly left with L. P. The next day, a social worker found the children at Clark's mother's house and took them to a hospital, where a physician discovered additional injuries suggesting child abuse. L. P. had a black eye, belt marks on his back and stomach, and bruises all over his body. A. T. had two black eyes, a swollen hand, and a large burn on her cheek, and two pigtails had been ripped out at the roots of her hair.

A grand jury indicted Clark on five counts of felonious assault (four related to A. T. and one related to L. P.), two counts of endangering children (one for each child), and two counts of domestic violence (one for each child). At trial, the State introduced L. P.'s statements to his teachers as evidence of Clark's guilt, but L. P. did not testify. Under Ohio law, children younger than 10 years old are incompetent to testify if they "appear incapable of receiving just impressions of the facts and transactions respecting which they are examined, or of relating them truly." After conducting a hearing, the trial court concluded that L. P. was not competent to testify. But under Ohio Rule of Evidence 807, which allows the admission of reliable hearsay by child abuse victims, the court ruled that L. P.'s statements to his teachers bore sufficient guarantees of trustworthiness to be admitted as evidence.

Clark moved to exclude testimony about L. P.'s out-of-court statements under the Confrontation Clause. The trial court denied the motion, ruling that L. P.'s responses were not testimonial statements covered by the Sixth Amendment. The jury found Clark guilty on all counts except for one assault count related to A. T., and it sentenced him to 28 years' imprisonment. Clark appealed his conviction, and a state appellate court reversed on the ground that the introduction of L. P.'s out-of-court statements violated the Confrontation Clause.

In a 4-to-3 decision, the Supreme Court of Ohio affirmed. It held that, under this Court's Confrontation Clause decisions, L. P.'s statements qualified as testimonial because the primary purpose of the teachers' questioning "was not to deal with an existing emergency but rather to gather evidence potentially relevant to a subsequent criminal prosecution." The court noted that Ohio has a "mandatory reporting" law that requires certain professionals, including preschool teachers, to report suspected child abuse to government authorities. In the court's view, the teachers acted as agents of the State under the mandatory reporting law and "sought facts concerning past criminal activity to identify the person responsible, eliciting statements that 'are functionally identical to live, in-court testimony, doing precisely what a witness does on direct examination.'"

We granted certiorari, and we now reverse.

II A

The Sixth Amendment's Confrontation Clause, which is binding on the States through the Fourteenth Amendment, provides: "In all criminal prosecutions, the accused shall enjoy the right . . . to be confronted with the witnesses against him." In Ohio v. Roberts, 448 U. S. 56, 66 (1980), we interpreted the Clause to permit the admission of out-of- court statements by an unavailable witness, so long as the statements bore "adequate 'indicia of reliability.'" Such indicia are present, we held, if "the evidence falls within a firmly rooted hearsay exception" or bears "particularized guarantees of trustworthiness."

In Crawford v. Washington, 541 U. S. 36 (2004), we adopted a different approach. We explained that "witnesses," under the Confrontation Clause, are those "who bear testimony," and we defined "testimony" as "a solemn declaration or affirmation made for the purpose of establishing or proving some fact." The Sixth Amendment, we concluded, prohibits the introduction of testimonial statements by a non-testifying witness, unless the witness is "unavailable to testify, and the defendant had had a prior opportunity for cross-examination." Applying that definition to the facts in Crawford, we held that statements by a witness during police questioning at the station house were testimonial and thus could not be admitted. But our decision in Crawford did not offer an exhaustive definition of "testimonial" statements.

Instead, Crawford stated that the label "applies at a minimum to prior testimony at a preliminary hearing, before a grand jury, or at a former trial; and to police interrogations."

Our more recent cases have labored to flesh out what it means for a statement to be "testimonial." In Davis v. Washington and Hammon v. Indiana, 547 U.S. 813 (2006), which we decided together, we dealt with statements given to law enforcement officers by the victims of domestic abuse. The victim in Davis made statements to a 911 emergency operator during and shortly after her boyfriend's violent attack. In Hammon, the victim, after being isolated from her abusive husband, made statements to police that were memorialized in a "'battery affidavit.'"

We held that the statements in Hammon were testimonial, while the statements in Davis were not. Announcing what has come to be known as the "primary purpose" test, we explained: "Statements are non-testimonial when made in the course of police interrogation under circumstances objectively indicating that the primary purpose of the interrogation is to enable police assistance to meet an ongoing emergency. They are testimonial when the circumstances objectively indicate that there is no such ongoing emergency, and that the primary purpose of the interrogation is to establish or prove past events potentially relevant to later criminal prosecution." Because the cases involved statements to law enforcement officers, we reserved the question whether similar statements to individuals other than law enforcement officers would raise similar issues under the Confrontation Clause.

In Michigan v. Bryant, 562 U. S. 344 (2011), we further expounded on the primary purpose test. The inquiry, we emphasized, must consider "all of the relevant circumstances." And we reiterated our view in Davis that, when "the primary purpose of an interrogation is to respond to an 'ongoing emergency,' its purpose is not to create a record for trial and thus is not within the scope of the Confrontation Clause." At the same time, we noted that "there may be other circumstances, aside from ongoing emergencies, when a statement is not procured with a primary purpose of creating an out-of-court substitute for trial testimony." "The existence vel non of an ongoing emergency is not the touchstone of the testimonial inquiry." Instead, "whether an ongoing emergency exists is simply one factor . . . that informs the ultimate inquiry regarding the 'primary purpose' of an interrogation."

One additional factor is "the informality of the situation and the interrogation." A "formal station house interrogation," like the questioning in Crawford, is more likely to provoke testimonial statements, while less formal questioning is less likely to reflect a primary purpose aimed at obtaining testimonial evidence against the accused. And in determining whether a statement is testimonial, "standard rules of hearsay, designed to identify some statements as reliable, will be relevant."

In the end, the question is whether, in light of all the circumstances, viewed objectively, the "primary purpose" of the conversation was to "create an out-of-courtsubstitute for trial testimony."

Applying these principles in Bryant, we held that the statements made by a dying victim about his assailant were not testimonial because the circumstances objectively indicated that the conversation was primarily aimed at quelling an ongoing emergency, not establishing evidence for the prosecution. Because the relevant statements were made to law enforcement officers, we again declined to decide whether the same analysis applies to statements made to individuals other than the police.

Opinion of the Court

Thus, under our precedents, a statement cannot fall within the Confrontation Clause unless its primary purpose was testimonial. "Where no such primary purpose exists, the admissibility of a statement is the concern of state and federal rules of evidence, not the Confrontation Clause." But that does not mean that the Confrontation Clause bars every statement that satisfies the "primary purpose" test. We have recognized that the Confrontation Clause does not prohibit the introduction of out-of-court statements that would have been admissible in a criminal case at the time of the founding. Thus, the primary purpose test is a necessary, but not always sufficient, condition for the exclusion of out-of-court statements under the Confrontation Clause.

B

In this case, we consider statements made to preschool teachers, not the police. We are therefore presented with the question we have repeatedly reserved: whether statements to persons other than law enforcement officers are subject to the Confrontation Clause.

Because at least some statements to individuals who are not law enforcement officers could conceivably raise confrontation concerns, we decline to adopt a categorical rule excluding them from the Sixth Amendment's reach.

Nevertheless, such statements are much less likely to be testimonial than statements to law enforcement officers. And considering all the relevant circumstances here, L. P.'s statements clearly were not made with the primary purpose of creating evidence for Clark's prosecution. Thus, their introduction at trial did not violate the Confrontation Clause. L. P.'s statements occurred in the context of an ongoing emergency involving suspected child abuse. When L. P.'s teachers noticed his injuries, they rightly became worried that the 3-year-old was the victim of serious violence. Because the teachers needed to know whether it was safe to release L. P. to his guardian at the end of the day, they needed to determine who might be abusing the child.2 Thus, the immediate concern was to protect a vulnerable child who needed help. Our holding in Bryant is instructive. As in Bryant, the emergency in this case was ongoing, and the circumstances were not entirely clear. L. P.'s teachers were not sure who had abused him or how best to secure his safety. Nor were they sure whether any other children might be at risk. As a result, their questions and L. P.'s answers were primarily aimed at identifying and ending the threat. Though not as harried, the conversation here was also similar to the 911 call in Davis.

The teachers' questions were meant to identify the abuser in order to protect the victim from future attacks. Whether the teachers thought that this would be done by apprehending the abuser or by some other means is irrelevant. And the circumstances in this case were unlike the interrogation in Hammon, where the police knew the identity of the assailant and questioned the victim after shielding her from potential harm.

There is no indication that the primary purpose of the conversation was to gather evidence for Clark's prosecution. On the contrary, it is clear that the first objective was to protect L. P. At no point did the teachers inform L. P. that his answers would be used to arrest or punish his abuser. L. P. never hinted that he intended his statements to be used by the police or prosecutors. And the conversation between L. P. and his teachers was informal and spontaneous. The teachers asked L. P. about his injuries immediately upon discovering them, in the informal setting of a preschool lunchroom and classroom, and they did so precisely as any concerned citizen would talk to a child who might be the victim of abuse. This was nothing like the formalized station-house questioning in Crawford or the police interrogation and battery affidavit in Hammon.

L. P.'s age fortifies our conclusion that the statements in question were not testimonial. Statements by very young children will rarely, if ever, implicate the Confrontation Clause.

Few preschool students understand the details of our criminal justice system. Rather, "research on children's understanding of the legal system finds that" young children "have little understanding of prosecution." And Clark does not dispute those findings. Thus, it is extremely unlikely that a 3-year-old child in L. P.'s position would intend his statements to be a substitute for trial testimony. On the contrary, a young child in these circumstances would simply want the abuse to end, would want to protect other victims, or would have no discernible purpose at all.

As a historical matter, moreover, there is strong evidence that statements made in circumstances similar to those facing L. P. and his teachers were admissible at common law. ("The Old Bailey" court in 18th-century London "tolerated flagrant hearsay in rape prosecutions involving a child victim who was not competent to testify because she was too young to appreciate the significance of her oath"). And when 18th-century courts excluded statements of this sort, they appeared to do so because the child should have been ruled competent to testify, not because the statements were otherwise inadmissible. It is thus highly doubtful that statements like L. P.'s ever would have been understood to raise Confrontation Clause concerns. Neither Crawford nor any of the cases that it has produced has mounted evidence that the adoption of the Confrontation Clause was understood to require the exclusion of evidence that was regularly admitted in criminal cases at the time of the founding. Certainly, the statements in this case are nothing like the notorious use of ex parte examination in Sir Walter Raleigh's trial for treason, which we have frequently identified as "the principal evil at which the Confrontation Clause was directed."

Finally, although we decline to adopt a rule that statements to individuals who are not law enforcement officers are categorically outside the Sixth Amendment, the fact that L. P. was speaking to his teachers remains highly relevant. Courts must evaluate challenged statements in context, and part of that context is the questioner's identity. Statements made to someone who is not principally charged with uncovering and prosecuting criminal behavior are significantly less likely to be testimonial than statements given to law enforcement officers. It is common sense that the relationship between a student and his teacher is very different from that between a citizen and the police. We do not ignore that reality. In light of these circumstances, the Sixth Amendment did not prohibit the State from introducing L.P.'s statements at trial.

III

Clark's efforts to avoid this conclusion are all off-base. He emphasizes Ohio's mandatory reporting obligations, in an attempt to equate L. P.'s teachers with the police and their caring questions with official interrogations. But the comparison is inapt. The teachers' pressing concern was to protect L. P. and remove him from harm's way. Like all good teachers, they undoubtedly would have acted with the same purpose whether or not they had a state-law duty to report abuse. And mandatory reporting statutes alone cannot convert a conversation between a concerned teacher and her student into a law enforcement mission aimed primarily at gathering evidence for a prosecution.

It is irrelevant that the teachers' questions and their duty to report the matter had the natural tendency to result in Clark's prosecution. The statements at issue in Davis and Bryant supported the defendants' convictions, and the police always have an obligation to ask questions to resolve ongoing emergencies. Yet, we held in those cases that the Confrontation Clause did not prohibit introduction of the statements because they were not primarily intended to be testimonial. Thus, Clark is also wrong to suggest that admitting L. P.'s statements would be fundamentally unfair given that Ohio law does not allow incompetent children to testify. In any Confrontation Clause case, the individual who provided the out-of-court statement is not available as an in-court witness, but the testimony is admissible under an exception to the hearsay rules and is probative of the defendant's guilt. The fact that the witness is unavailable because of a different rule of evidence does not change our analysis.

Finally, Clark asks us to shift our focus from the context of L. P.'s conversation with his teachers to the jury's perception of those statements. Because, in his view, the "jury treated L. P.'s accusation as the functional equivalent of testimony," Clark argues that we must prohibit its introduction. Brief for Respondent 42.

Our Confrontation Clause decisions, however, do not determine whether a statement is testimonial by examining whether a jury would view the statement as the equivalent of in-court testimony.

The logic of this argument, moreover, would lead to the conclusion that virtually all out-of-court statements offered by the prosecution are testimonial. The prosecution is unlikely to offer out-of-court statements unless they tend to support the defendant's guilt, and all such statements could be viewed as a substitute for in-court testimony. We have never suggested, however, that the Confrontation Clause bars the introduction of all out-of-court statements that support the prosecution's case. Instead, we ask whether a statement was given with the "primary purpose of creating an out-of-court substitute for trial testimony." Bryant, supra, at 358. Here, the answer is clear: L. P.'s statements to his teachers were not testimonial.

IV

We reverse the judgment of the Supreme Court of Ohio and remand the case for further proceedings not inconsistent with this opinion.

It is so ordered.
Cite as: 576 U. S. ____ (2015)
SCALIA, J., concurring in judgment
OHIO, PETITIONER v. DARIUS CLARK
ON WRIT OF CERTIORARI TO THE SUPREME COURT OF OHIO
June 18, 2015
JUSTICE SCALIA, with whom JUSTICE GINSBURG joins, concurring in the judgment.

I agree with the Court's holding, and with its refusal to decide two questions quite unnecessary to that holding: what effect Ohio's mandatory-reporting law has in trans forming a private party into a state actor for Confrontation Clause purposes, and whether a more permissive Confrontation Clause test—one less likely to hold the statements testimonial—should apply to interrogations by private actors. The statements here would not be testimonial under the usual test applicable to informal police interrogation.

L. P.'s primary purpose here was certainly not to invoke the coercive machinery of the State against Clark. His age refutes the notion that he is capable of forming such a purpose. At common law, young children were generally considered incompetent to take oaths, and were therefore unavailable as witnesses unless the court determined the individual child to be competent. The inconsistency of L. P.'s answers—making him incompetent to testify here—is hardly unusual for a child of his age. And the circumstances of L. P.'s statements objectively indicate that even if he could, as an abstract matter, form such a purpose, he did not. Nor did the teachers have the primary purpose of establishing facts for later prosecution. Instead, they sought to ensure that they did not deliver an abused child back into imminent harm. Nor did the conversation have the requisite solemnity necessary for testimonial statements. A 3-year-old was asked questions by his teachers at school. That is far from the surroundings adequate to impress upon a declarant the importance of what he is testifying to.

That is all that is necessary to decide the case, and all that today's judgment holds.

I write separately, however, to protest the Court's shoveling of fresh dirt upon the Sixth Amendment right of confrontation so recently rescued from the grave in Crawford v. Washington, 541 U. S. 36 (2004). For several decades before that case, we had been allowing hearsay statements to be admitted against a criminal defendant if they bore "'indicia of reliability.'" Ohio v. Roberts, 448 U. S. 56, 66 (1980). Prosecutors, past and present, love that flabby test. Crawford sought to bring our application of the Confrontation Clause back to its original meaning, which was to exclude unconfronted statements made by witnesses—i.e., statements that were testimonial. 541 U. S., at 51. We defined testimony as a " 'solemn declaration or affirmation made for the purpose of establishing or proving some fact,'" ibid.—in the context of the Confrontation Clause, a fact "potentially relevant to later criminal prosecution,"

Crawford remains the law. But when else has the categorical overruling, the thorough repudiation, of an earlier line of cases been described as nothing more than "adopting a different approach," ante, at 4—as though Crawford is only a matter of twiddle-dum twiddle-dee

preference, and the old, pre-Crawford "approach" remains available? The author unabashedly displays his hostility to Crawford and its progeny, perhaps aggravated by inability to muster the votes to overrule them. Crawford "does not rank on the author of the opinion's top-ten list of favorite precedents—and ... the author could not restrain himself from saying (and saying and saying) so."

But snide detractions do no harm; they are just indications of motive. Dicta on legal points, however, can do harm, because though they are not binding, they can mislead. Take, for example, the opinion's statement that the primary-purpose test is merely one of several heretofore unmentioned conditions ("necessary, but not always sufficient") that must be satisfied before the Clause's protections apply. That is absolutely false and has no support in our opinions. The Confrontation Clause categorically entitles a defendant to be confronted with the witnesses against him; and the primary-purpose test sorts out, among the many people who interact with the police informally, who is acting as a witness and who is not. Those who fall into the former category bear testimony, and are therefore acting as "witnesses," subject to the right of confrontation. There are no other mysterious requirements that the Court declines to name.

The opinion asserts that future defendants, and future Confrontation Clause majorities, must provide "evidence that the adoption of the Confrontation Clause was understood to require the exclusion of evidence that was regularly admitted in criminal cases at the time of the founding." This dictum gets the burden precisely backwards—which is of course precisely the idea.

Defendants may invoke their Confrontation Clause rights once they have established that the state seeks to introduce testimonial evidence against them in a criminal case without unavailability of the witness and a previous opportunity to cross-examine.

The burden is upon the prosecutor who seeks to introduce evidence over this bar to prove a long-established practice of introducing specific kinds of evidence, such as dying declarations, see Crawford, supra, at 56, n. 6, for which cross-examination was not typically necessary. A suspicious mind (or even one that is merely not naïve) might regard this distortion as the first step in an attempt to smuggle longstanding hear say exceptions back into the Confrontation Clause—in other words, an attempt to return to Ohio v. Roberts.

But the good news is that there are evidently not the votes to return to that halcyon era for prosecutors; and that dicta, even calculated dicta, are nothing but dicta. They are enough, however, combined with the peculiar phenomenon of a Supreme Court opinion's aggressive hostility to precedent that it purports to be applying, to prevent my joining the writing for the Court. I concur only in the judgment.

Cite as: 576 U. S. (2015)
THOMAS, J., concurring in judgment
SUPREME COURT OF THE UNITED STATES
No. 13–1352
OHIO, PETITIONER v. DARIUS CLARK
ON WRIT OF CERTIORARI TO THE SUPREME COURT OF OHIO June 18, 2015
JUSTICE THOMAS, concurring in the judgment.

I agree with the Court that Ohio mandatory reporters are not agents of law enforcement, that statements made to private persons or by very young children will rarely implicate the Confrontation Clause, and that the admission of the statements at issue here did not implicate that constitutional provision. I nonetheless cannot join the majority's analysis. In the decade since we first sought to return to the original meaning of the Confrontation Clause, we have carefully reserved consideration of that Clause's application to statements made to private persons for a case in which it was squarely presented.

This is that case; yet the majority does not offer clear guidance on the subject, declaring only that "the primary purpose test is a necessary, but not always sufficient, condition" for a statement to fall within the scope of the Confrontation Clause. Ante, at 7. The primary purpose test, however, is just as much "an exercise in fiction . . . disconnected from history" for statements made to private persons as it is for statements made to agents of law enforcement, if not more so. I would not apply it here. Nor would I leave the resolution of this important question in doubt.

Instead, I would use the same test for statements to private persons that I have employed for statements to agents of law enforcement, assessing whether those statements bear sufficient indicia of solemnity to qualify as testimonial.

This test is grounded in the history of the common-law right to confrontation, which "developed to target particular practices that occurred under the English bail and committal statutes passed during the reign of Queen Mary, namely, the civil-law mode of criminal procedure, and particularly its use of ex parte examinations as evidence against the accused." Reading the Confrontation Clause in light of this history, we have interpreted the accused's right to confront "the witnesses against him," as the right to confront those who "bear testimony" against him, C(relying on the ordinary meaning of "witness"). And because "testimony . . . is . . . a solemn declaration or affirmation made for the purpose of establishing or proving some fact," an analysis of statements under the Clause must turn in part on their solemnity. I have identified several categories of extrajudicial statements that bear sufficient indicia of solemnity to fall within the original meaning of testimony. Statements "contained in formalized testimonial materials, such as affidavits, depositions, prior testimony, or confessions" easily qualify. And statements not contained in such materials may still qualify if they were obtained in "a formalized dialogue"; after the issuance of the warnings required by Miranda v. Arizona, 384 U. S. 436 (1966); while in police custody; or in an attempt to evade confrontation.

That several of these factors seem inherently inapplicable to statements made to private persons does not mean that the test is unsuitable for analyzing such statements. All it means is that statements made to private persons rarely resemble the historical abuses that the common-law right to confrontation developed to address, and it is those practices that the test is designed to identify.

Here, L. P.'s statements do not bear sufficient indicia of solemnity to qualify as testimonial. They were neither contained in formalized testimonial materials nor obtained as the result of a formalized dialogue initiated by police. Instead, they were elicited during questioning by L. P.'s teachers at his preschool. Nor is there any indication that L. P.'s statements were offered at trial to evade confrontation. To the contrary, the record suggests that the prosecution would have produced L. P. to testify had he been deemed competent to do so. His statements bear no "resemblance to the historical practices that the Confrontation Clause aimed to eliminate." Ibid. The admission of L. P.'s extrajudicial statements thus does not implicate the Confrontation Clause.

I respectfully concur in the judgment.

LEGAL GLOSSARY

Acquittal - A jury verdict that a criminal defendant is not guilty, or the finding of a judge that the evidence is insufficient to support a conviction.

Active judge - A judge in the full-time service of the court. Compare to senior judge. **Admissible** - A term used to describe evidence that may be considered by a jury or

judge in civil and criminal cases.
Affidavit - A written or printed statement made under oath.

Affirmed - In the practice of the court of appeals, it means that the court of appeals has concluded that the lower court decision is correct and will stand as rendered by the lower court.

Alternate juror - A juror selected in the same manner as a regular juror who hears all the evidence but does not help decide the case unless called on to replace a regular juror.

Amicus curiae - Latin for "friend of the court." It is advice formally offered to the court in a brief filed by an entity interested in, but not a party to, the case.

Appeal - A request made after a trial by a party that has lost on one or more issues that a higher court review the decision to determine if it was correct. To make such a request is "to appeal" or "to take an appeal." One who appeals is called the "appellant;" the other party is the "appellee."

Appellant - The party who appeals a district court's decision, usually seeking reversal of that decision.

Appellate - About appeals; an appellate court has the power to review the judgment of a lower court (trial court) or tribunal. For example, the U.S. circuit courts of appeals review the decisions of the U.S. district courts.

Appellee - The party who opposes an appellant's appeal, and who seeks to persuade the appeals court to affirm the district court's decision.

Arraignment - A proceeding in which a criminal defendant is brought into court, told of the charges in an indictment or information, and asked to plead guilty or not guilty.

Assets - Property of all kinds, including real and personal, tangible and intangible. **Assume** - An agreement to continue performing duties under a contract or lease.

Attorney-client privilege - The protection that applicable law provides for confidential attorney-client communications

Bail - The release, prior to trial, of a person accused of a crime, under specified conditions designed to assure that person's appearance in court when required. Also, can refer to the amount of bond money posted as a financial condition of pretrial release.

Bench trial - A trial without a jury, in which the judge serves as the factfinder.

Brief - A written statement submitted in a trial or appellate proceeding that explains one side's legal and factual arguments.

Burden of proof - The duty to prove disputed facts. In civil cases, a plaintiff generally has the burden of proving his or her case. In criminal cases, the government has the burden of proving the defendant's guilt. *(See standard of proof.)*

Capital offense - A crime punishable by death.

Case file - A complete collection of every document filed in court in a case.

Case law - The law as established in previous court decisions. A synonym for legal precedent. Akin to common law, which springs from tradition and judicial decisions.

Caseload - The number of cases handled by a judge or a court. **Chambers** - The offices of a judge and his or her staff.

Character - A person's credit, character, honor, reputation, and/or good name

Clerk of court - The court officer who oversees administrative functions, especially managing the flow of cases through the court. The clerk's office is often called a court's central nervous system.

Common law - The legal system that originated in England and is now in use in the United States, which relies on the articulation of legal principles in a historical succession of judicial decisions. Common law principles can be changed by legislation.

Community service - A special condition the court imposes that requires an individual to work — without pay — for a civic or nonprofit organization.

Concurrent sentence - Prison terms for two or more offenses to be served at the same time, rather than one after the other. Example: Two five-year sentences and one three-year sentence, if served concurrently, result in a maximum of five years behind bars.

Consecutive sentence - Prison terms for two or more offenses to be served one after the other. Example: Two five-year sentences and one three-year sentence, if served consecutively, result in a maximum of 13 years behind bars.

Conviction - A judgment of guilt against a criminal defendant.
Counsel - Legal advice; a term also used to refer to the lawyers in a case.

Count - An allegation in an indictment or information, charging a defendant with a crime. An indictment or information may contain allegations that the defendant committed more than one crime. Each allegation is referred to as a count.

Court - Government entity authorized to resolve legal disputes. Judges sometimes use "court" to refer to themselves in the third person, as in "the court has read the briefs."

Court reporter - A person who makes a word-for-word record of what is said in court, generally by using a stenographic machine, shorthand or audio recording, and then produces a transcript of the proceedings upon request.

Declarant - The person who made the statement.

De facto - Latin, meaning "in fact" or "actually." Something that exists in fact but not as a matter of law.

De jure - Latin, meaning "in law." Something that exists by operation of law.

De novo - Latin, meaning "anew." A trial de novo is a completely new trial. Appellate review de novo implies no deference to the trial judge's ruling.

Defendant - In a criminal case, the person accused of the crime.

Deposition - An oral statement made before an officer authorized by law to administer oaths. Such statements are often taken to examine potential witnesses, to obtain discovery, or to be used later in trial. See discovery.

Discovery - Procedures used to obtain disclosure of evidence before trial.

Docket - A log containing the complete history of each case in the form of brief chronological entries summarizing the court proceedings.

Due process - In criminal law, the constitutional guarantee that a defendant will receive a fair and impartial trial.

Duplicate - Means a counterpart produced by a mechanical, photographic, chemical, electronic, or other equivalent process or technique that accurately reproduces the original.

En banc - French, meaning "on the bench." All judges of an appellate court sitting together to hear a case, as opposed to the routine disposition by panels of three judges. In the Ninth Circuit, an en banc panel consists of 11 randomly selected judges.

Evidence - Information presented in testimony or in documents that is used to persuade the fact finder (judge or jury) to decide the case in favor of one side or the other.

Ex parte - A proceeding brought before a court by one party only, without notice to or challenge by the other side.

Expert witness - A person who is permitted to testify at a trial because of special knowledge or proficiency in a particular field that is relevant to the case.

Exclusionary rule - Doctrine that says evidence obtained in violation of a criminal defendant's constitutional or statutory rights is not admissible at trial.

Exculpatory evidence - Evidence indicating that a defendant did not commit the crime.

Federal public defender - An attorney employed by the federal courts on a full-time basis to provide legal defense to defendants who are unable to afford counsel. The judiciary administers the federal defender program pursuant to the Criminal Justice Act.

Felony - A serious crime, usually punishable by at least one year in prison.
File - To place a paper in the official custody of the clerk of court to enter into the files or records of a case.

Grand jury - A body of 16-23 citizens who listen to evidence of criminal allegations, which is presented by the prosecutors, and determine whether there is probable cause to believe an individual committed an offense.

Habeas corpus - Latin, meaning "you have the body." A writ of habeas corpus generally is a judicial order forcing law enforcement authorities to produce a prisoner they are holding, and to justify the prisoner's continued confinement. Federal judges receive petitions for a writ of habeas corpus from state prison inmates who say their state prosecutions violated federally protected rights in some way.

Hearsay - A statement outside of the current trial or hearing that a party offers in evidence to prove the truth of the matter asserted in the statement. Evidence presented by a witness who did not see or hear the incident in question but heard about it from someone else. With some exceptions, hearsay generally is not admissible as evidence at trial

Home confinement - A special condition the court imposes that requires an individual to remain at home except for certain approved activities such as work and medical appointments. Home confinement may include the use of electronic monitoring equipment – a transmitter attached to the wrist or the ankle – to help ensure that the person stays at home as required.

Hypothetical - A conceptual imagining of circumstances, that if true, would explain certain facts.

Impeachment - The process of calling a witness's testimony into doubt. For example, if the attorney can show that the witness may have fabricated portions of his testimony, the witness is said to be "impeached"

In camera - Latin, meaning in a judge's chambers. Often means outside the presence of a jury and the public. In private.

Inculpatory evidence - Evidence indicating that a defendant did commit the crime.

Indictment - The formal charge issued by a grand jury stating that there is enough evidence that the defendant committed the crime to justify having a trial; it is used primarily for felonies. See also information.

Information - A formal accusation by a government attorney that the defendant committed a misdemeanor. See also indictment.

Judge - An official of the Judicial branch with authority to decide lawsuits brought before courts. Used generically, the term judge may also refer to all judicial officers, including Supreme Court justices.

Jurisdiction - The legal authority of a court to hear and decide a certain type of case. It also is used as a synonym for venue, meaning the geographic area over which the court has territorial jurisdiction to decide cases.

Jurisprudence - The study of law and the structure of the legal system

Jury - The group of persons selected to hear the evidence in a trial and render a verdict on matters of fact. See also grand jury.

Jury instructions - A judge's directions to the jury before it begins deliberations regarding the factual questions it must answer and the legal rules that it must apply.

Lay witness - A witness who is not an expert. Lay witnesses may not offer opinions, unless they are based on firsthand knowledge or help to clarify testimony.

Misdemeanor - An offense punishable by one year of imprisonment or less. See also felony.

Mistrial - An invalid trial, caused by fundamental error. When a mistrial is declared, the trial must start again with the selection of a new jury.

Moot - Not subject to a court ruling because the controversy has not actually arisen, or has ended

Motion - A request by a litigant to a judge for a decision on an issue relating to the case.

Motion in Limine - A pretrial motion requesting the court to prohibit the other side from presenting, or even referring to, evidence on matters said to be so highly prejudicial that no steps taken by the judge can prevent the jury from being unduly influenced.

Nolo contendere - No contest. A plea of nolo contendere has the same effect as a plea of guilty, as far as the criminal sentence is concerned, but may not be considered as an admission of guilt for any other purpose.

Opinion - A belief or judgment short of absolute conviction, certainty, or positive knowledge; it is a conclusion that certain facts are probably true. A Judge's written explanation of the decision of the court. Because a case may be heard by three or more judges in the court of appeals, the opinion in appellate decisions can take several forms. If all the judges completely agree on the result, one judge will write the opinion for all. If all the judges do not agree, the formal decision will be based upon the view of the majority, and one member of the majority will write the opinion. The judges who did not agree with the majority may write separately in dissenting or concurring opinions to present their views. A dissenting opinion disagrees with the majority opinion because of the reasoning and/or the principles of law the majority used to decide the case. A

concurring opinion agrees with the decision of the majority opinion but offers further comment or clarification or even an entirely different reason for reaching the same result. Only the majority opinion can serve as binding precedent in future cases. See also precedent.

Oral argument - An opportunity for lawyers to summarize their position before the court and also to answer the judges' questions.

Original - An original of a writing or recording means the writing or recording itself or any counterpart intended to have the same effect by the person who executed or issued it. For electronically stored information, "original" means any printout, or other output readable by sight, if it accurately reflects the information. An "original" of a photograph includes the negative or a print from it.

Parole - The release of a prison inmate – granted by the U.S. Parole Commission – after the inmate has completed part of his or her sentence in a federal prison. When the parolee is released to the community, he or she is placed under the supervision of a U.S. probation officer.

The Sentencing Reform Act of 1984 abolished parole in favor of a determinate sentencing system in which the sentence is set by sentencing guidelines. Now, without the option of parole, the term of imprisonment the court imposes is the actual time the person spends in prison.

Pendency - A state of being undecided, the state of an action after it has begun, and before it has been decided

Peremptory challenge - A district court may grant each side in a civil or criminal trial the right to exclude a certain number of prospective jurors without cause or giving a reason.

Photograph - Means a photographic image or its equivalent stored in any form. **Plea** - In a criminal case, the defendant's statement pleading "guilty" or "not guilty" in

answer to the charges. See also nolo contendere.

Pleadings - Written statements filed with the court that describe a party's legal or factual assertions about the case.

Precedent - A court decision in an earlier case with facts and legal issues similar to a dispute currently before a court. Judges will generally "follow precedent" - meaning that they use the principles established in earlier cases to decide new cases that have similar facts and raise similar legal issues. A judge will disregard precedent if a party can show that the earlier case was wrongly decided, or that it differed in some significant way from the current case.

Presentence report - A report prepared by a court's probation officer, after a person has been convicted of an offense, summarizing for the court the background information needed to determine the appropriate sentence.

Pretrial conference - A meeting of the judge and lawyers to plan the trial, to discuss which matters should be presented to the jury, to review proposed evidence and witnesses, and to set a trial schedule. Typically, the judge and the parties also discuss the possibility of settlement of the case.

Pretrial services - A function of the federal courts that takes place at the very start of the criminal justice process – after a person has been arrested and charged with a federal crime and before he or she goes to trial. Pretrial services officers focus on investigating the backgrounds of these persons to help the court determine whether to release or detain them while they await trial. The decision is based on whether these individuals are likely to flee or pose a threat to the community. If the court orders release, a pretrial services officer supervises the person in the community until he or she returns to court.

Pro se - Representing oneself. Serving as one's own lawyer.

Pro tem - Temporary.

Probation - Sentencing option in the federal courts. With probation, instead of sending an individual to prison, the court releases the person to the community and orders him or her to complete a period of supervision monitored by a U.S. probation officer and to abide by certain conditions.

Probation officer - Officers of the probation office of a court. Probation officer duties include conducting presentence investigations, preparing presentence reports on convicted defendants, and supervising released defendants.

Procedure - The rules for conducting a lawsuit; there are rules of civil procedure, criminal procedure, evidence, bankruptcy, and appellate procedure.

Prosecute - To charge someone with a crime. A prosecutor tries a criminal case on behalf of the government

Public document - Document such as court records, deeds, and public registers authenticated by a public officer and made available for public reference and use

Record - A written account of the proceedings in a case, including all pleadings, evidence, and exhibits submitted in the course of the case.

Recording - Consists of letters, words, numbers, or their equivalent recorded in any manner.

Relevant evidence - Evidence and testimony directly relating to the issues disputed or discussed

Remand - Send back.

Reverse - The act of a court setting aside the decision of a lower court. A reversal is often accompanied by a remand to the lower court for further proceedings.

Self-authenticating - Authorship or origin is conclusively or unquestionably established on its face

Sentence - The punishment ordered by a court for a defendant convicted of a crime.

Sentencing guidelines - A set of rules and principles established by the United States Sentencing Commission that trial judges use to determine the sentence for a convicted defendant.

Sequester - To separate. Sometimes juries are sequestered from outside influences during their deliberations.

Service of process - The delivery of writs or summonses to the appropriate party.

Standard of proof - Degree of proof required. In criminal cases, prosecutors must prove a defendant's guilt "beyond a reasonable doubt." The majority of civil lawsuits require proof "by a preponderance of the evidence" (50 percent plus), but in some the standard is higher and requires "clear and convincing" proof.

Statement - A person's oral assertion, written assertion, or nonverbal conduct, if the person intended it as an assertion.

Statute - A law passed by a legislature.

Statute of limitations - The time within which a lawsuit must be filed, or a criminal prosecution begun. The deadline can vary, depending on the type of civil case or the crime charged.

Sua sponte - Latin, meaning "of its own will." Often refers to a court taking an action in a case without being asked to do so by either side.

Subpoena - A command, issued under a court's authority, to a witness to appear and give testimony.

Subpoena duces tecum - A command to a witness to appear and produce documents.

Temporary restraining order - Akin to a preliminary injunction, it is a judge's short- term order forbidding certain actions until a full hearing can be conducted. Often referred to as a TRO.

Testimony - Evidence presented orally by witnesses during trials or before grand juries.

Tort - A civil, not criminal, wrong. A negligent or intentional injury against a person or property, with the exception of breach of contract.

Transcript - A written, word-for-word record of what was said, either in a proceeding such as a trial, or during some other formal conversation, such as a hearing or oral deposition

Uphold - The appellate court agrees with the lower court decision and allows it to stand. See affirmed.

Ultimate issue - An Ultimate issue references a point that is not yet decided and is sufficient in itself or in connection with other points to resolve the entire case. Ultimate issue is sometimes referred to as ultimate question.

Venue - The geographic area in which a court has jurisdiction. A change of venue is a change or transfer of a case from one judicial district to another.

Verdict - The decision of a trial jury or a judge that determines the guilt or innocence of a criminal defendant, or that determines the final outcome of a civil case.

Voir dire - Jury selection process of questioning prospective jurors, to ascertain their qualifications and determine any basis for challenge.

Warrant - Court authorization, most often for law enforcement officers, to conduct a search or make an arrest.

Witness - A person who has knowledge of an event by seeing it. A person called upon by either side in a lawsuit to give testimony before the court or jury.

Work-product protection - The protection that applicable law provides for tangible material (or its intangible equivalent) prepared in anticipation of litigation or for trial

Writ - A written court order directing a person to take, or refrain from taking, a certain act.

Writ of certiorari - An order issued by the U.S. Supreme Court directing the lower court to transmit records for a case which it will hear on appeal.

Writing - Consists of letters, words, numbers, or their equivalent set down in any form.

www.ingramcontent.com/pod-product-compliance
Lightning Source LLC
Chambersburg PA
CBHW070728220326
41598CB00024BA/3344